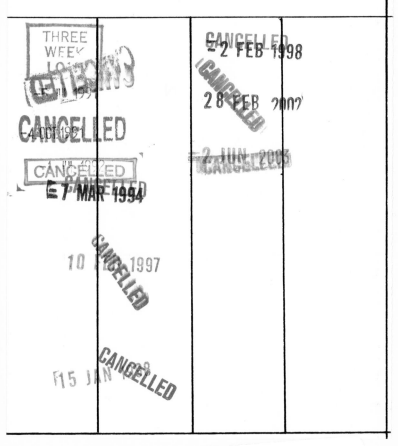

By the same author:

Characters of Joyce

DAVID G. WRIGHT

Yeats's Myth of Self: The Autobiographical Prose

GILL AND MACMILLAN

BARNES & NOBLE BOOKS
Totowa, New Jersey

Published in Ireland by
Gill and Macmillan Ltd
Goldenbridge
Dublin 8
with associated companies in
Auckland, Dallas, Delhi, Hong Kong,
Johannesburg, Lagos, London, Manzini,
Melbourne, Nairobi, New York, Singapore,
Tokyo, Washington
© David G. Wright 1987
7171 1537 2
Print origination in Northern Ireland by Textflow Services, Belfast
Printed in Great Britain by The Camelot Press, Southampton

British Library Cataloguing in Publication Data
Wright, David G.
Yeats's myth of self: the autobiographical prose.
1. Yeats, W. B.—Prose
I. Title
828'.808   PR5906.A3
ISBN 0-7171-1537-2

First published in the USA 1988 by
BARNES & NOBLE BOOKS
81 ADAMS DRIVE
TOTOWA, NEW JERSEY, 07512
ISBN: 0-389-20760-8

Library of Congress Cataloguing in Publication Data
Wright, David G.
Yeats's Myth of Self:

Bibliography: 2pp.
Includes index.
1. Yeats, W. B. (William Butler), 1865–1939—Biography.
2. Yeats, W. B. (William Butler), 1865–1939—Prose.
3. Autobiography.
4. Authors, Irish—19th Century—Biography—History and Criticism.
5. Authors, Irish—20th Century—Biography—History and Criticism.
I. Title.
PR5906.W75 1987 821'.8 [B] 87–14504
ISBN 0-389-20760-8

This is not an autobiographical novel:
It is about some *other* portly, dissolute, immoral and
middle-aged art-dealer.

Kyril Bonfiglioli, *Don't Point that Thing at Me*

We can study files for decades, but every so often
we are tempted to throw up our hands
and declare that history is merely another literary genre:
the past is autobiographical fiction pretending
to be a parliamentary report.

Julian Barnes, *Flaubert's Parrot*

Contents

Preface

THIS book grew from my fascination with Yeats's ingenious ways of enticing readers to participate in his self-depiction and self-creation. In other words, I am interested in the rhetorical strategies which he uses in his autobiographical prose to draw us towards particular impressions of his life—even while we may imagine that he is simply and objectively narrating events which had once occurred in the real world.

Some of the book's distant origins go back as far as my doctoral dissertation ('Autobiographical Expression in Yeats and Joyce', University of Toronto, 1978), and I remain indebted to Michael J. Sidnell for his shrewd supervision of that project. Earlier versions of two sections have appeared as articles, and I am grateful to the editors who have permitted me to draw on this material; specifically, to John H. Sutherland for my 'Behind the Lines: Strategies of Self-Portraiture in Yeats and Joyce' (*Colby Library Quarterly*, 16 [1980], 148–57), which lies behind the present Chapter 8, and to Kathleen Quinn Zsamar for my 'Yeats as a Novelist' (*Journal of Modern Literature*, 12 [1985], 261–76; copyright Temple University), which is an earlier version of part of the present Chapter 2.

I am indebted to the copyright holders of the texts from which I have quoted. Extracts from W.B. Yeats's *Autobiographies* (copyright 1916, 1936 by the Macmillan Publishing Company, renewed 1944, 1964 by Bertha George Yeats) are reprinted with permission of the Macmillan Publishing Company and of A.P. Watt Ltd. on behalf of Michael B. Yeats and Macmillan (London) Ltd.

I should also like to express gratitude to my colleagues and students at the University of Auckland, many of whom have found themselves obliged, at various times, to discuss my ideas about Yeats's writings.

D. G. W.
Auckland
April 1987

LIST OF ABBREVIATIONS

The following abbreviations are used for citations of works by Yeats, and for Wade's bibliography of Yeats's works and his edition of Yeats's letters:

A	*Autobiographies*. London: Macmillan, 1955.
B	Wade, Allan. *A Bibliography of the Writings of W. B. Yeats*. 3rd ed. Rev. and ed. Russell K. Alspach. London: Hart-Davis, 1968.
CP	*The Collected Poems of W. B. Yeats*. London: Macmillan, 1950.
CPL	*The Collected Plays of W. B. Yeats*. London: Macmillan, 1952.
E&I	*Essays and Introductions*. London: Macmillan, 1961.
JS	*John Sherman and Dhoya*. Ed. Richard J. Finneran. Detroit: Wayne State Univ. Press, 1969.
L	*The Letters of W. B. Yeats*. Ed. Allan Wade. London: Hart-Davis, 1954.
M	*Memoirs*. Ed. Denis Donoghue. London: Macmillan, 1972.
MY	*Mythologies*. London: Macmillan, 1959.
SB	*The Speckled Bird*. Ed. William H. O'Donnell. Toronto: McClelland & Stewart, 1976.
1AV	*A Vision*. London: T. Werner Laurie, 1925.
2AV	*A Vision*. Rev. ed. London: Macmillan, 1937.

Full bibliographical details for other works cited or consulted appear in the Bibliography. To avoid clutter and duplication, these details are omitted in the text and notes.

ONE

Thinking about Autobiography

AUTOBIOGRAPHY today is under siege. Many recent philosophers and literary critics have questioned our faith in individuality, integrated personality and the literary transmission of facts—all beliefs on which autobiographical writing seems to depend. Some theoretical writers claim that recording the history of a unique self reflects misunderstanding of human nature and of literary processes. Attempts to communicate the nature of the individual self defy widespread recent scepticism about authorial intention and the text's relationship to external reality.

Autobiographical writing as we know it is also a recent phenomenon. Before the eighteenth century, most people who wrote about their lives had a specific religious, didactic or apologetic purpose: to teach others how to live, or to justify their own spiritual experiences. Detailed records of writers' lives, published simply because the authors wished to write them, became common at about the same time as the novel. They often seem to share with the novel various humanist beliefs about the importance of individual experience, beliefs which flourish in particular societies and at particular times. Contemporary society may be moving away from such values, towards a structure in which people become increasingly interchangeable components. The kinds of meaning which most autobiographers have attempted to give to their lives in recording them rest on assumptions of psychological coherence and authorial omnipotence which are not absolute, and which remain open to question.

At the same time, however, numerous theoretical writings about autobiography have appeared. These writings have sometimes been prompted by critical attacks made on the genre, though they have not necessarily answered those attacks on a philosophical level. Their proliferation nevertheless emphasises the volatility of our current assumptions.[1] While stressing that autobiography remains a respectable and vital form of literature, most theorists treat problems which arise not from the metaphysics of individual selfhood but, more narrowly, from the intricate mechanics of literary self-depiction. Many writers have stressed the problematic position of autobiographical activity, poised between a theoretical obligation to adhere to facts and the constant likelihood (some would say necessity) of veering towards fiction. Elizabeth W. Bruss claims that autobiographical work is 'viable only when one recognizes that it creates truth as much as expresses it'; she adds that 'no autobiographer ought to depict himself without first becoming aware of how much fiction is implicit in the idea of a "self" '.[2]

Theorists frequently insist that autobiographical writing involves the creation of an approximation of the true past, not that past itself. The true past no longer exists, and *as* the past, it never did exist; only the present exists, together with documents and memories which hint at what the past might once have been like. The interpretative problems posed by all history and biography are much more extreme in the case of autobiographical writing because of the special relationship which links the self writing with the self described. This relationship involves access to private information, since we all have a few secrets unknown to anyone else. The relationship is also swayed by the temptations of vanity and masochism, of patronage and revenge, of special pleading; 'every middle-aged man conducts a mildly indecent love affair with the young man he once was'.[3]

The question of fact and fiction in autobiographical writing has been addressed by practising autobiographers and novelists as well as by critics. Vladimir Nabokov, who remarks on his penchant for bestowing an autobiographical detail on a fictional character as if it were a medal, wryly insinuates himself into works not ostensibly autobiographical, then turns back to admonish 'a certain type of critic who when reviewing a work of fiction keeps dotting all the i's with the author's head'.[4] He hints to readers embarking on his novel *Glory* that apparent parallels with his autobiography *Speak, Memory* are unimportant. The awareness of such writers that autobiography is problematic does not, of course, mean that we should believe everything they say about their own practice in the genre, and the frequent attempts made by these writers to confuse the issue have their own rhetorical (and sometimes autobiographical) purposes.

Popular fascination with autobiographical writing continues apparently unabated, despite critical attempts either to question its right to exist or to emphasise its literary complexities or implausibilities. Readers are drawn to autobiographies partly because verbal recapitulation of the personal past remains a universal phenomenon. We are all autobiographers, whether deliberate or otherwise. Self-consciousness demands that we reflect constantly on our experience, and various influences—conventions of conversation, assumptions about causality, even familiarity with narrative literature—converge to shape our thoughts into linear accounts of the past. Whether we grandly write 'my autobiography' after an eminent career or merely describe a few hours' events after an ordinary day, we are forever reconstructing our experience in verbal form. Even Roland Barthes, once a leader of the structuralist movement which professed scepticism about this mode of self-expression, wrote an autobiography; it is highly idiosyncratic, but for that very reason it asserts individuality, something which all autobiographical activity seeks to do. In addition to curiosity about autobiographers' circumstances—which itself may chiefly reflect interest in affinities or contrasts between their lives and our own lives—we are also fascinated by the very process of self-depiction. We may secretly hope that autobiographers' attempts to make sense of their lives will help us to make sense of our own.

Readers of autobiography, then, seldom trouble themselves with philosophical doubts about its theoretical validity. Most readers also free themselves from the problem of fact and fiction which concerns the theorist: they readily accept that autobiographers sometimes fail to tell the truth, or even attempt to deceive. A few readers will make a point of trying to catch the autobiographer off guard in the act of concealment or distortion, but this partial kind of reading rests on the questionable assumption that objective truth can ever be firmly established by extra-textual means. As critics we may wish to consider such external information, and banning it altogether would be the same kind of deterministic error as applying it too strenuously; but its application should form only one of a range of possible analytic methods. Most readers of autobiographies presumably approach with a more balanced mixture of curiosity, scepticism and, perhaps, self-interest.

Popular responses to autobiographical texts, though often more enthusiastic, are not necessarily superior to those of theorists or critics. Autobiographical writing remains a self-conscious and artful genre, as the theorists have helped to demonstrate, and it requires subtle responses from the reader. The philosophical gap between reader and theorist may be wider in the case of autobiographical texts than in any other literary field. Although the active role of the reader of fiction is now taken for granted and receives increasing attention, the reader of autobiographical writing seems to be envisaged in criticism as a relatively passive creature. This emphasis seems surprising if we bear in mind not only the current popularity of autobiographies—presumably, if readers seek out a book energetically they will also read it energetically—but also those aspects of autobiography to which the theorists themselves have directed most attention, particularly its fictive, imaginative and rhetorical dimensions.

The reader's involvement in the literary techniques of the autobiographer therefore seems a vital matter which is often neglected. Readers may sometimes underestimate an autobiographer's conscious efforts to create a particular image of the self. In terms of literary responses (as distinct from a desire for facts) this problem has nothing to do with the 'reliability' of an autobiographer's discourse. It does concern the method, the adequacy, and the sensitivity of our interpretation.

Autobiographical writing is always an imaginative enterprise, and must be read as such, whether particular readers or writers consider this requirement consciously or not. The desire to appear in a certain way, to emphasise a chosen dimension of the life, may override any aim to show the facts. Writers may openly acknowledge the relativity of autobiographical reality, and operate accordingly; or they may pretend that all is impartial truth, yet still manipulate our responses by more oblique means. The autobiographer cannot perceive facts objectively, but must rely to some extent on memory, a notoriously inconsistent witness to earlier events (being based firmly in the present, like everything living, not in the past as we sometimes seem to believe). The autobiographer operates in a radically different world from the biographer, who should presumably attempt to be as impartial and 'factual' as possible.

Given the impossibility of complete objectivity and the limitations of memory, only the imagination can make the perilous leap from the present self to the past self, over a gap further widened by each intervening experience—including the experience of attempted recollection. The more often we try to recall a past incident, the more radically we are likely to alter its shape. Having had an experience, we differ from our state before or during that experience, and knowing retrospection can never simulate quite successfully an original innocent response or an emotion like anxiety. Yet if something disappears in the transformation, something may also be gained by the superimposition of two evaluations. As T. S. Eliot remarks, we will often feel that

> We had the experience but missed the meaning,
> And approach to the meaning restores the experience
> In a different form.[5]

Autobiographical writing seeks pattern. Where no structure spontaneously appears in a recalled life, structure may need to be imposed artificially. Thus the events of the past will be in turn heightened and reduced, juxtaposed for comparison, and reshaped. Turning points and moments of revelation often achieve in retrospect an intensity which they lacked while being experienced. Even if it is true that

> Knowledge imposes a pattern, and falsifies,
> For the pattern is new in every moment
> And every moment is a new and shocking
> Valuation of all we have been,[6]

an attempt can still be made to shape the past by literary means.

The pattern an autobiographer creates from the events of the past life may, therefore, differ from the outline which a biographer would perceive in it. The autobiographer may see experiences dominated and shaped by a particular aspect of the past—family, religion, education, talent—or may wish to concentrate on an intangible aspect of development rather than on the events which other people see in the life. Such selectivity should be accepted as an indication of what the autobiographer considers important, such an indication constituting, in itself, an autobiographical statement.

If the autobiographer stresses inner development, as imaginative authors usually do, external circumstances of the life may be radically altered in the retelling. Like Harry in Eliot's *The Family Reunion*, autobiographers may fear that they will be misunderstood:

> All that I could hope to make you understand
> Is only events: not what has happened.
> And people to whom nothing has ever happened
> Cannot understand the unimportance of events.[7]

Contingency ('events') may have to be cleared away in order that the true outline of the life ('what has happened') may emerge for the reader. Intellectual development may be stressed by omitting to mention a family background or a marriage, for example.

A fictional character combines fragments of the author's experience, thought and imagination, magnetised into unity by aesthetic need; but so does an account of the writer's own past. Like a novelist, an autobiographical writer constructs personae to carry the narrative. The central persona will have a special relationship to the autobiographer, but it is always wise to investigate what kind of 'I' is selected, how consistently the persona is presented, and whether a single or multiple persona is used. An autobiographical text containing a multiple persona, one which serves different needs in different parts of the work, demands special treatment. The relationship between persona and reader may also be problematic or fluctuating. Even in autobiographical texts written without close attention to philosophical matters, the relations among author, persona and reader may be complex: 'Rousseau taught subsequent novelists . . . that even with the literal identity of subject and narrator, the mere span of time separating the two provides sufficient distance to allow for all the potentially ironical divergence in point of view between character and narrator that a novelist could require'.[8]

An autobiographer may seek symbolic, metaphorical analogues for past life rather than attempting to express that life directly. Metaphor and symbol, which work to make private experiences seem more public, help to bridge the gap between present and past, and enable us to perceive affinities between earlier and later selves or understand differences between them. The partial selves selected by many autobiographers (the poet, the public figure), and the partial phases or dimensions of life chosen by others (childhood, artistic achievement) become metaphorical or metonymic representations of the whole self.

If metaphor establishes a connection, irony seems to repudiate one, though it may do so only in order to direct our attention to a more important connection elsewhere. Irony serves to keep the reader or persona at a precise distance from the present self, and to achieve control over moments of rapprochement or estrangement. Irony seems particularly crucial in autobiographical writing because of the special relationship linking author and persona; ironical incursions interrupting this relationship, though in fact quite common, probably have more effect on readers in autobiographical writing than similar techniques would have elsewhere.

Thus various literary methods offer themselves to the autobiographer. They may include attempts to impose pattern on discrete particulars, selectivity (the decision to include certain phases or aspects of the life and exclude others), deliberate analogies with and borrowings from the techniques of overtly fictional works (mostly novels), and the use of persona, metaphor and irony. All these techniques may be used to guide the reader's response in a chosen direction.

The boundaries of autobiographical endeavour, then, are ever shifting. Attempts to classify 'true autobiography' can produce lines of demarcation which puncture the works under study rather than separating them. A satisfactory formal definition of autobiography must account for the inclusion of a

wide array of materials. On the other hand, significant autobiographical acts may take place in novels and other literary
arenas. The formal intention of writing 'my autobiography'
may curtail revelations which could only be made fully in a less
deliberate context. Formal autobiography may even distort the
true relationship between a witness and an experience, a
relationship which more fluid texts might reproduce with
greater fidelity.

André Gide suggests in his autobiography *Si le grain ne meurt*
that 'memoirs are never more than half sincere, however great
the concern for truth: everything is always more complicated
than it is said to be. Perhaps we even approach truth more
closely in the novel'.[9] Gide acknowledges, indeed, that some of
the material to be presented in his autobiography has already
appeared in his novels. Novelists who write declared autobiographies may be tempted to record their lives fitfully through
an exaggerated sense of obligation to facts. If such novelists
instead wrote novels which reflected the coherence of their
experiences, those 'fictional' works might claim to be a more
truthful account than a declared autobiography could ever
have provided. If such a novel falsified the contingency of life, it
might yet reproduce faithfully the artist's quest for order, which
may transcend in significance the details which become distorted in the course of the quest. The truth of the life may seem to
reside in what the artist has made rather than in what has been
given. A fictional account may thus symbolise, as well as
embody, the artist's desire to take sole responsibility for truth.
If the novel was a flirtation or battle with reality, the autobiography might rather seem an attempt to lock reality away, and
the tensions and energies of life would thus survive better in the
novel. No part of experience, in any case, need be irrelevant to
an account of a life, and nothing in fiction can be separated
completely from experience. In other words, the relationship
between subject and form may be as flexible in autobiographical writing as in any other mode.

Nevertheless, all autobiographical writing shares common
features. It always postulates a particular, unique consciousness which parallels that of the author, and it attempts self-
definition by contrast: 'I am I because I differ from them.' It
usually appeals to our parallel sense of the uniqueness of our

own experiences. It always treats themes of growth and development. The autobiographical self never appears static, as a
more fully novelistic character may: it requires momentum to
remain aloft. That element of a novelistic character which
undergoes the most marked psychological development will
often be autobiographical in origin, since we can never be as
intensely aware of other people's transitions and transformations as we are of our own. Autobiographical authors seek to
understand the forces which have made them what they are, to
revisit (sentimentally, curiously or in quest of what were once
alternative possibilities) the signposts pointing to their present
position, to recapture from time moments which seem to have
been stolen from them by the circumstances of their lives.

Autobiographical acts may occur in diaries, poems and even
plays, as well as in novels. (James Joyce's *Exiles* is a strikingly
revealing autobiographical play.) The novel, as an extended
prose narrative, nevertheless remains the most direct and
illuminating comparison to the typical declared autobiography. Yet it still seems necessary to insist on the special status of
the declared autobiography even as we acknowledge its ready
assimilation of fictional techniques. While we should approach
an autobiography with flexible expectations, they will still be
different expectations from those which we bring to other
genres. Autobiographical writing is a search for a particular
kind of truth, a truth which should be defined not by external
criteria but in terms of the coherence of the self portrayed. In
constructing a self to mould the attitudes of others, autobiographers also mould their own attitudes. Seeking truth, they create
it by their manner of approaching. Even while the structure of
autobiographical writing follows the contours of the author's
life, it also tends to shape them. By the use of telling, emblematic detail, imagery and metaphor, an autobiographer raises
events and personalities into symbolism, a symbolism which in
turn colours actual life. To know that one will write of an event
later may give that event a literary shape even as it occurs.
Thus life may be consciously directed in the service of art, and
so create the 'facts' on which that art can build.

This book investigates Yeats's *Autobiographies*, combining
this study with a preliminary and comparative inspection of his
two autobiographical novels, *John Sherman* and *The Speckled Bird*,

but passing over his autobiographical work in other genres. (This limitation to prose texts involves philosophical assumptions, but also more practical matters: judgments of scale, of the nature of the criticism which already exists, and of the varying usefulness of the comparisons to be drawn among different genres.) The final chapter considers Yeats's own attitudes to the autobiographical process, a necessary concern here since these views, besides being fascinating in themselves, are often presented within the text of *Autobiographies* itself. The question of Yeats's fidelity to fact in his autobiographical writing scarcely arises here, except where it casts light on internal contradictions or obscurities in the texts. Instead, this study attends to those questions about autobiographical expression which have been raised in this introduction.

Yeats's autobiography strikes most readers as a highly idiosyncratic, self-conscious and elusive one. Structurally, it challenges rigorous formal definitions of the genre, yet its diverse elements (whimsical interludes, quoted diary entries, protracted discussions of people other than Yeats, even brief critical essays and the text of a formal speech) are more than diversions or decorations: they form essential parts of Yeats's self-portrait, and their presence in itself makes a kind of autobiographical statement. The diverse components of the book, written in different styles at different times, implicitly acknowledge the changing shape of both self and self-conception, paralleling Yeats's transitions from dreamy young romantic to established middle-aged poet and dramatist, and then to literary elder statesman. The reader must reconstitute the central figure from these diverse components and so participate actively in the creation of Yeats's 'unity of being'.

Autobiographies also challenges other assumptions about author-text-reader relationships, and particularly about the possibility of the reader's imaginative identification with an autobiographical persona. The multiple persona serves markedly varied functions in different sections of the text. Especially in *The Trembling of the Veil*, the persona seems highly elusive, and the reader is prompted to investigate the reasons for so striking an autobiographical stance. Yeats also acknowledges the tendency of memory to create fictions; in prefacing *Reveries over Childhood and Youth* he writes 'I have changed nothing to my knowledge; and yet it must be that I have changed many things without my knowledge; for I am writing after many years and have consulted neither friend, nor letter, nor old newspaper, and describe what comes oftenest into my memory' (*A* 3). We are free to suspect that he has also changed some of his material deliberately, despite the insistent disclaimer.

Yeats's autobiography, for all its diversity, is carefully constructed and controlled. He may have written it partly because of his introspective nature and his self-conception as a poet of emotion and imagination, but he also wished to dictate in some detail the world's response to him. Sensing that other people's conceptions of his life were liable to error, he carefully constructed a Yeats able to stand against the assembled forces of misinterpretation. His autobiography records his own attempts to interpret his life, a more important record than a list of events could ever have been. Rather than depicting his experiences, *Autobiographies* shows the meanings he attempted to give them. He has been 'reborn as an idea, something intended, complete' (*E&I* 509) in the imagination of his readers. Because of the nature of Yeats's personality, it might have appeared that he had had the meaning and missed the experience—that all was re-evaluation, nothing immediate life. This danger is avoided in *Autobiographies*, partly through his willingness to include mundane details as well as erudite appraisals; the house-drains and central heating he mentions are as palpable as the spiritualism and nationalism.[10] Yet he also employs a range of more sophisticated and fascinating rhetorical techniques to make his readers into accomplices, and such techniques will be the chief concern of this book.

TWO

Autobiographical Fiction

YEATS'S two early novels, *John Sherman* and *The Speckled Bird*, do not reveal him as a great forgotten novelist, yet they have their own literary merit and considerable autobiographical interest (the literary merit certainly more conspicuous in *John Sherman*, the autobiographical interest perhaps greater in *The Speckled Bird*).[1] Only *John Sherman* was published by Yeats (in 1891, revised in 1908); *The Speckled Bird* defied his efforts to shape it, and the tangled manuscript had to wait until 1973 to be deciphered and published. *John Sherman* thus presents a more poised and polished image of Yeats's preoccupations, while *The Speckled Bird* shows a Yeats less firmly in control and prone to reveal his concerns indirectly. After *The Speckled Bird* Yeats never attempted sustained autobiographical fiction, but divided his attention between declared autobiography and miscellaneous short forms, such as the 'Michael Robartes' fragments.

Yeats's published comments on *John Sherman* are mostly light-hearted. 'I know I gained greatly from my experiment in novel writing. The hero turned out a bad character. . . . I am in hopes he may reform', he wrote to Katharine Tynan (*L* 123). The novel itself remains similarly light in tone, a comedy in mood as well as mode. Occasionally the comedy becomes self-conscious and heavy-handed, as in a description of a clothes-moth afflicted with apocalyptic anxieties, a passage which Yeats wisely excised in revision (*JS* 63). Such awkwardness reflects Yeats's occasional uncertainty about a reader's reactions to his humour; this particular passage precluded any reaction except embarrassment. Generally, though, humour in *John Sherman* remains lively and engaging: Margaret's spirited and vigorous flirtation with Sherman follows immediately her mother's lament that she is sadly pining away (*JS* 64), and Sherman's observation that Margaret's eyes seem 'to watch him from the flies upon the ceiling' (*JS* 66) falls ludicrously and parodically short of the romantic. Another amusing touch in *John Sherman* is the meaningless precision of the dates provided, such as '9th of December' (with no year specified) in the second line of the text (*JS* 43). Yeats may be making fun of his own carelessness about such matters; his letters and diary entries are dated vaguely or not at all, and he remarks in one letter that 'I long for a life without dates and without any settled abode' (*L* 551). In the 1891 text's introductory note 'Ganconagh', Yeats's pseudonymous narrator, contributes humour in his comment on the two works, *John Sherman* and *Dhoya*, which appear together in the volume: 'The first I do not care for because it deals with dull persons and the world's affairs, but the second has to do with my own people' (*JS* 39). This comment recalls Yeats's own disparaging remarks on the novel, but it also amuses us because *John Sherman* occupies nearly nine-tenths of the book. 'Ganconagh' has to suffer through a protracted tedious narrative exercise, as he sees it, in order to reach a brief account of his 'own people'.

Yeats recognised that novel-writing required not only humour, but also the depiction of 'character' and 'conversation'. *John Sherman* shows him working at such tasks earnestly but with apparent ease.

Most of his characters depend on living models. Yeats may have adopted this method as a direct and possibly retaliatory response to his father's insistence that he should write about real people rather than mythological beings. Nevertheless, some of these associations with authentic prototypes may have been exaggerated in criticism. Richard J. Finneran, for example, associates Mrs Sherman with Susan Yeats, the poet's mother.[2] While this suggested connection seems altogether unsurprising, little specific evidence for it exists. When Yeats wrote *John Sherman* his mother had already suffered the stroke which left her largely helpless and housebound for the rest of her life, while Sherman's mother seems moderately active and quite willing to travel, and this at a time when Sherman is considerably older than the Yeats writing the novel. Finneran stresses the love of both women for Sligo, but while such attachment may be well attested in the case of Susan Yeats, Mrs Sherman emphasises that she has no strong preferences at all about places to live, reminding her son 'I have often told you [that] I do not like one place better than another. I like them all equally little' (*JS* 53). Her son's plan that they should return from London to Ballah pleases her, but this pleasure springs from an attachment to the past rather than from fondness for any particular place: 'Her old home had long seemed to her a kind of lost Eden, where with she was accustomed to contrast the present. When, in time, this present had grown into the past it became an Eden in turn. She was always ready for a change, if the change came to her in the form of a return to something old' (*JS* 99). Yeats may have avoided attributing an attachment to Ballah to Mrs Sherman in order to stress that Sherman alone makes the decision to return there. Emphasis thus falls on Sherman's inner drama.

Margaret Leland cannot be based on observation of Maud Gonne, whom Yeats, at the time he wrote *John Sherman*, had yet to meet. (But the Margaret in *The Speckled Bird*, who resembles the one in *John Sherman*, does assimilate a few of Maud Gonne's characteristics and several images which Yeats repeatedly associated with her.) Margaret in *John Sherman* can also be associated, as William M. Murphy has shown, with the headstrong Laura Armstrong, who was apparently the girl Yeats mentions (without naming) in *Reveries over Childhood and Youth*, whose confidant and undeclared lover he became (*A* 76).[3]

Mary Carton seems to derive her name from Mary Cronan, to whom Yeats wrote at least one letter in about 1884 (*L* 30). She may owe more to this source; evidence is lacking. Murphy also associates Mary Carton with Katharine Tynan. A comment by Yeats which has been published in *Memoirs* gives limited support to this identification: 'I wrote many letters to Katharine Tynan, a very plain woman, and one day I over-heard somebody say that she was the kind of woman who might make herself very unhappy about a man. I began to wonder if she was in love with me and if it was my duty to marry her. Sometimes when she was in Ireland, I in London would think it possible that I should, but if she came to stay, or I saw her in Ireland, it became impossible again' (*M* 32). It has been claimed that Yeats did, in fact, propose to her.[4] Yet considerable differences in personality seem to distinguish the quiet, dutiful Mary Carton from the Katharine Tynan who went on to write innumerable novels and who had already engaged Yeats in lively correspondence (none of it really supporting the notion that she was the kind of woman who might make herself very unhappy about a man, though we cannot disprove Yeats's claim that he thought she was). Yeats may have borrowed a few aspects of his relationship with her without taking much of her personality.

Murphy plausibly offers a model for William Howard in the scholar Edward Dowden's brother John, who was a curate in Sligo (which he disliked) and later a bishop in Edinburgh. He had difficulties with his congregations because of his insistence on intellectual independence. These suggested connections seem convincing enough, though Yeats never knew John Dowden personally. Murphy has traced other traits and ideas of Howard's to various sources, including J. B. Yeats; such composite origins might help to explain Howard's slippery, even self-contradictory, character—a character which nevertheless functions successfully in the novel as a foil to Sherman's attempts to achieve unity.

Numerous minor connections link Yeats's characters with real people. Murphy's article points out several of these relationships, though Finneran had earlier identified Michael Sherman (John Sherman's uncle) with William Pollexfen (Yeats's grandfather), both men being taciturn co-directors of shipping companies. Murphy adds that in creating the firm of Sherman and Saunders, ship-brokers, Yeats combined an echo of the name of one Pollexfen enterprise (Middleton and Pollexfen) with the business of another (the Sligo Steam Navigation Company). Several critics have seen John Sherman himself as a portrait of Henry Middleton, Yeats's cousin; Sherman's indolence and fondness for fishing, in particular, have been traced to this source.

The most interesting connections between characters in *John Sherman* and living people, however, are the directly autobiographical ones. These connections, involving chiefly John Sherman and William Howard, need to be precisely defined. Yeats remarked in a letter that (despite his father's warnings) he had had difficulty preventing his characters from becoming eastern symbolic monsters, exactly what he had wanted to avoid in moving from *Dhoya* to *John Sherman* (*L* 92); he also took pains to ensure that they would not appear too simply or too neatly as aspects of himself.

Thus Sherman, while he shares Yeats's tendency to write with great effort, hardly seems 'poetical', as Finneran claims. His gardening and office work do not suggest the Yeats of the 1880s; later Yeats would complain in a poem about the 'boredom of the desk or of the spade' (*CP* 385). Mary Carton falls short of Yeats's romantic ideal as he had envisaged it in *The Wanderings of Oisin* through Oisin's love for Niamh, or as it was to be partly realised in Maud Gonne. Howard, the High-Church curate, always appears vaguely ridiculous, while Yeats's self-image was basically serious, and Howard also seems a pale version of the Anti-self compared with later, spirited figures like Cuchulain. Howard falls easy prey to Sherman's scheme to bring him and Margaret together; as a 'man of action' he is comically flawed.

Nevertheless, these characters do clearly assimilate aspects of Yeats, and he does use them for a project of self-analysis and self-depiction which anticipates modes he will adopt later in writing *Autobiographies*. The polarity between Sherman and Howard also anticipates the divisions between Yeats's characters Michael Robartes and Owen Aherne. Sherman embodies—and exaggerates—Yeats's dreamy, impractical side. He shares Yeats's revery of escaping to an island in a lake near Sligo (the island, thinly disguised as Inniscrewin in the 1891 text, boldly appears as Innisfree in 1908), and has Yeats's general preference for Sligo (Ballah in the novel) over London. Sherman's feelings on approaching Ballah by sea may be safely taken as autobiographical (*JS* 101–2). Sherman and his mother settle in Hammersmith, where Yeats went to school (*JS* 60; we may compare the account Yeats gives in *Reveries over Childhood and Youth*, *A* 32). Howard, by contrast to Sherman, feels at home in London, where Yeats would later live for many years. Howard enjoys urban society and glamour, while Sherman chooses to settle in a small town with the unprepossessing if virtuous Mary Carton; Howard's inclinations thus anticipate Yeats's life in the years which followed the writing of the novel more precisely than Sherman's own choices do. Howard expresses the difference between himself and Sherman in a metaphor which seems beyond his own imaginative power but entirely Yeatsian: 'Your mind and mine are two arrows. Yours has got no feathers, and mine has no metal on the point' (*JS* 95). The image of Sherman as a featherless arrow anticipates an account of himself which Yeats gives in *The Trembling of the Veil*: 'At seventeen years old I was already an old-fashioned brass cannon full of shot, and nothing had kept me from going off but a doubt as to my capacity to shoot straight' (*A* 116). In the Preface which he added to *John Sherman* in 1908, Yeats explicitly acknowledges the association between Sherman and himself, as well as implying that between Sherman and Henry Middleton.

Yeats thus uses both Sherman and Howard to enact a drama of self-presentation. While detailed resemblances between their lives and Yeats's life are limited, the notion of ambivalence and of self-contradiction conveyed through the two complementary figures seems typically Yeatsian.

The notion of self-division appears not only in the contrast between Sherman and Howard but also in antitheses within Sherman, conveyed in the games of chess he plays against himself, right hand against left. Although he ultimately decides for Ballah and for Mary Carton, London and Margaret Leland also attract him for a time. Sherman must balance the conflicting claims of contentment with one's present lot and ambition to improve it, realism and idealism, utility and pleasure. This last antithesis finds symbolic expression in his garden, rigidly divided between vegetables and flowers (*JS* 51), as well as in his relationships with Mary and with Margaret, the teacher and the tennis-player. Sherman senses that to be contented people require 'some occupation peculiar to the place' (*JS* 46)—fishing symbolises this requirement for him, as it will later do for Yeats—but he also feels the obligation to seek wider experience. The kind of self-division we see in Sherman has some positive connotations, however, for all Yeats's lamentation about his own lack of 'unity of being'. Self-division seems superior to the glib juxtaposition of contraries of which Howard shows himself capable; Howard even boasts 'do I not combine perfectly the zealot with the man of the world?' (*JS* 93). Nevertheless, Sherman does achieve a degree of harmony at the end by renouncing the London world and settling in Ballah, where 'he had found his centre of unity' (*JS* 104). He is able to emerge on one side of the debate and find relative contentment, while Howard takes over the London/Margaret side of his life; the fact that Yeats bases Howard as well as Sherman on his own being may suggest that he feels no such escape from ambivalence to be possible for himself.

Yeats may not have anticipated that sources for his characters, and connections between his characters' lives and his own life, would be pursued with the unblinking obsessiveness of modern literary scholarship. Yet he himself provides clues to the personal dimension of *John Sherman*, notably in the 1908 Preface. He must have realised that informed readers would perceive the novel as a treatment of his own psychological landscape, whether or not they knew of the detailed associations which existed between the fiction and the fact. This realisation contributes to the coy, slightly flirtatious tone of the novel (a tone which, of course, also suits the mood of much of the action): Yeats plays with our curiosity about his life and perceptions, as he also does throughout *Autobiographies*.

Apart from the ambivalences and antitheses embodied in the characters, other autobiographical concerns are conveyed in *John Sherman* by structural and textual means. The novel contains considerable dramatic irony, for example, and besides contributing to humour it serves to illuminate Sherman's slowly growing self-awareness by contrasting his own sense of his position with the impressions we are able to form about his progress. The torn-up letter Sherman discovers, which turns out when he reassembles it to contain Margaret's vacuous musings about her romantic life, precipitates his proposal to her even while it displays for us her true, rather chilly character (*JS* 69–70). It seems possible that the letter was deliberately planted by Margaret to ensnare Sherman, and if so, it amusingly anticipates the stratagem which he will employ later to get rid of Margaret. (If the letter was not deliberately planted by Margaret, it was deliberately and brazenly planted by Yeats, and we are meant to 'reconstruct' meanings from it, just as Sherman does.) Dramatic irony also appears in Sherman's early prediction 'I am not . . . the kind of person who falls in love inconveniently' (*JS* 47), and in Mrs Sherman's remark that Howard 'might do very well . . . for one of those Carton girls at the rectory' (*JS* 50).

Perhaps the most impressive aspect of *John Sherman* is its apparently effortless use of imagery and symbolism, arts which Yeats was simultaneously using to advantage in *The Wanderings of Oisin*. As in many of his poems, the images and symbols serve to bridge the gap between private and public realms by giving to personal preoccupations a wider resonance. Yeats's autobiographical energies in *John Sherman* may have been as fully employed in manipulating these methods of referring experience outwards as in the depiction of characters based on himself.

Occasionally Yeats comments explicitly, within the text itself, on his manner of using symbols. When Sherman goes into his garden he carries a book of travels and a trowel, representing his dreamy reflections on faraway places and his attachment to the immediate and everyday (*JS* 50). (The close competition between these interests may even be suggested by the verbal resemblance between 'travel' and 'trowel'.) He receives a letter from his businessman uncle in London, which represents Sherman's concern about his rather aimless present life and his sense that he might improve himself by going elsewhere to work. Yeats glosses the meaning of such symbols: 'It will now be seen why the garden, the book, and the letter were the three symbols of his life, summing up as they did his love of out-of-door doings, his meditations, his anxieties. His life in the garden had granted serenity to his forehead, the reading of his few books had filled his eyes with reverie, and the feeling that he was not quite a good citizen had given a slight and occasional trembling to his lips' (*JS* 51–2).

Yeats uses many of his symbols and images less self-consciously than he does here, however. Some of them act as subtle, oblique glosses on Sherman's actions and decisions. Imagery of gates, locks and keys becomes explicitly sexual in accounts of Sherman and Margaret: 'The Square gate brought them to a stop. It was locked, but she had the key. The lock was stiff, but turned easily for John Sherman' (*JS* 65). This passage suggests that Margaret would be an easy conquest for Sherman, but is not suited to him. When Sherman is with Mary

Carton, images of gates and walls sometimes take on more Edenic connotations; after Sherman tells Mary of his engagement to Margaret, 'without a word, locking the door behind them, they went out' (*JS* 81). Moments later, 'they parted; the gate in the wall closed behind her'. On his return to Ballah, Sherman says to Mary 'We will surround ourselves with a wall. The world will be on the outside, and on the inside we and our peaceful lives' (*JS* 107). Thus he proposes to return to the Eden which Ballah, at this moment, represents for him. Earlier, when she had first advised Sherman to go to London, thus possibly sacrificing her love for him, Mary had remarked 'There! I have raked the fire out. We must not forget to lock the door behind us' (*JS* 57). The symbolism of suppressed passion and denial of the past is clear in this case.

These examples serve to juxtapose more pointedly Sherman's two relationships, with Margaret and with Mary. Other images which comment on Sherman's situation involve animals. The blind dog chasing rabbits shows the danger that pursuit of poorly perceived goals will be delusory and futile, and Yeats emphasises the parallel with Sherman heavily; the animal appears as 'a dog of his acquaintance' (*JS* 53), and on leaving the field the dog accompanies Sherman, so that 'they came together to the rectory'. The rabbits are the dog's 'form of the eternal chimera'. The dog will be echoed by the black cat which Sherman sees chasing its own shadow (*JS* 68–9) and with which he is also closely associated.

A further array of animal and plant images conveys particular positive and negative implications, especially implications of fertility or sterility. Numerous birds appear in *John Sherman*, as in *The Wanderings of Oisin* and the opening scene of *The Speckled Bird*. In London, where the bushes are 'covered with dust' (*JS* 77), the sparrows are 'ruffling their feathers'; when Sherman returns to Ballah, by contrast, he notices 'the ceaseless chirruping of the sparrows in the ivy outside' (*JS* 80), and during his night of self-revelation which will culminate in Mary's acceptance of his proposal 'a number of small birds rose chirruping from where they had been clinging among the reeds' (*JS* 111). In *Oisin*, too, Yeats contrasts singing birds with ruffling ones, with the same connotations of fecund life and dusty sterility which he introduces into the novel. Similarly, there is a contrast between the generally sterile plant life of London and the fecundity of Ballah. Sherman's garden in London contains 'a single tall pear tree that never bore fruit' (*JS* 60). The novel records that 'Sherman planted and dug and raked this pocket-handkerchief of a garden most diligently, rooting out the docks and dandelions and mouse-ear and the patches of untimely grass. . . . [But] it was far too small and unfertile and shaded-in to satisfy his love of gardener's experiments and early vegetables. Perforce this husbandry was too little complex for his affections to gather much round plant and bed. His garden in Ballah used to touch him like the growth of a young family' (*JS* 70–71). When he returns to Ballah he sees Mary Carton's 'prints of fruits and leaves and bird-nests' (*JS* 79). Seeds are also mentioned often. Sherman sorts seeds while contemplating his future (*JS* 52), as if to dramatise the various possible outcomes of present choices. Later, sensing his entrapment in London, he feels that he is one of those 'whose granaries are in the past' (*JS* 77). Yet when he declares his affection for Mary, a 'bird shook a shower of seed on his shoulder' (*JS* 108), a positive sign which seemingly obliterates the sterile 'shower of new sovereigns' (*JS* 70) Sherman had envisaged when he was first engaged to Margaret. In a final instance of botanical symbolism, Sherman imagines his old, discarded thoughts as dead leaves.

A light-hearted application of symbolism appears in the chess game which Sherman plays with Howard, where 'Sherman relied most upon his bishops and queen' while 'Howard was fondest of the knights' (*JS* 94). The bishops and queen may be associated with Howard (who, Sherman says, can 'hope to die a bishop' [*JS* 96]) and Margaret, with whom Sherman is also conducting a game. The knight's oblique move suits Howard's sense of his own slyness (an ironical sense, given Sherman's manipulation of his actions), and he also sees himself as a knight, one who rescues damsels in distress.[5] Another jocular application of symbolism appears when Sherman, meditating about a sketching technique taught to children, tries to fit squares into pictures of cows (*JS* 85)—an attempt to impose abstraction or theory onto life, a mistake which he has made previously.

These symbols and images range from the central to the

peripheral, from the poignant to the comic. But they all help to give the story substance, to show that the situations depicted refer to more than merely themselves, and to bridge the gap between Sherman's experiences and those experiences which are likely to be brought to the novel by its readers. The basic plot of *John Sherman*, involving an exchange of lovers and the correction of misalliances, is conventional enough, but by the use of symbol and image Yeats both gives the plot a specific location (in terms of the Ballah-London polarity, for example) and boldly reinforces its universal overtones (by using archetypes such as symbols of fertility and of frustration). These techniques are perhaps the most sophisticated devices used in *John Sherman*, which for all its overtones remains a simple story by Yeats's standards, and they give it a density of reference it would lack without them.

Yeats, then, intends his self-depiction in *John Sherman* to be attached both to real places and to shared social assumptions. It is not a profoundly confessional novel, nor one which heavily emphasises the uniqueness of his own experiences (*The Speckled Bird* will be closer to this position). But it does exploit autobiographical methods which Yeats will use again later in his more 'factual' accounts of his past.

The humour and ironic detachment of *John Sherman*, for example, help Yeats to control aesthetic distance, protecting his own personality from excessive involvement in the fiction. The use of a pseudonymous narrator in the first edition no doubt helped this process of detachment, though 'Ganconagh' could be speaking for Sherman when he says 'I care for nothing in the world but love and idleness' (*JS* 39). (The disguise, in any case, was always thin since a poem included in *Dhoya* had already appeared elsewhere under Yeats's own name.) Humour and ironic detachment are qualities which Yeats seems to need most urgently when writing autobiographically; they appear strongly in *John Sherman* and in *Autobiographies*, but are not especially prominent elsewhere in Yeats. Their scarcity in *The Speckled Bird* may help to explain, or may be partly explained by, Yeats's dissatisfaction with that work.

John Sherman concerns itself with the definition of identity. It exploits techniques of character-contrast which Yeats would develop later and which appear in most autobiographical writing, where there is often a need to contrast the authorial persona with other people. Sherman comes to feel that his sense of identity depends on affinities with a particular place and its values, a realisation which coincides and is synonymous with his discovery that he loves Mary Carton: his 'sense of personal identity' is 'disturbed by [the] sudden revelation' of his love for her (*JS* 81).

Polarised values in *John Sherman* dramatise the need to choose between alternatives, to find a place to which to fasten one's allegiances. Yeats's quibbles on the implications of 'home' (*JS* 82) illustrate this quandary. Sherman, like Yeats, faces the problem of defining his true home, in an imaginative as well as a literal sense. Difficult choices, conflicting allegiances, appear in *John Sherman* as inescapable aspects of the search for the meaning of experience.

For all its humour and irony, then, *John Sherman* uses its fictions seriously in a quest for the nature of selfhood. Sherman, admittedly, achieves this quest in a way which Yeats could hardly have wished for himself: life in Ballah with Mary Carton, one suspects, would not have satisfied him for long. Yet this very discrepancy, this need to keep Sherman at a suitable fictive distance, anticipates the strategies Yeats will use in later autobiographical works. He aims not to confess his experiences but to control his depiction of them.

The Speckled Bird, Yeats's other autobiographical novel, poses considerable problems to its readers, as it did to its writer. Yeats found himself unable either to finish the novel or to abandon it, as in the same years he could neither consummate nor relinquish his relationship with Maud Gonne; later he found himself unable either to destroy the novel or to offer it to a publisher. In *Autobiographies* he calls *The Speckled Bird* 'a novel that I could neither write nor cease to write which had Hodos Chameliontos for its theme' (*A* 376); he continues 'My chief person was to see all the modern visionary sects pass before his bewildered eyes, as Flaubert's Saint Anthony saw the Christian sects, and I was as helpless to create artistic, as my chief person to create philosophic, order'.

A preliminary text of *The Speckled Bird* was published in 1973 and a more comprehensive one in 1976, both edited by William H. O'Donnell. O'Donnell has identified four distinct 'versions' of the novel and includes them all in his 1976 edition, though only two of these, the 'Final' and 'De Burgh' texts, approach novel length; the other two are fragments. The 'Final' and 'De Burgh' versions resemble one another, as the earlier 'Leroy' and 'Island' versions resemble one another, but many differences exist between the two earlier and the two later versions, so that the third ('De Burgh') text is virtually a new work. Yeats kept changing the surname of the novel's protagonist and his father, trying 'De Burgh', 'Leroy' and 'Hearne' in different versions. These changes may reflect some reluctance to characterise the family (the three names imply different social classes, for example). The name 'Hearne' appears only in the 'Final' version, as does the allusion to the speckled bird, and there is a clear relationship between the allusion and the name: Hearne obviously suggests 'hern', the alternative spelling for 'heron', a spelling which Yeats uses frequently elsewhere; the relationship can be confirmed from Yeats's other works where herns and herons appear. In all versions, however, the protagonist is called Michael and his father is called John; the girl admired or loved by Michael, generally at a distance, appears as Margaret in every text except the 'Island' version, where she is Oonah.[6]

When Yeats began work on *The Speckled Bird* it would have been natural for him to look back at his one previous (and also autobiographical) novel *John Sherman*, as Dickens in beginning work on *Great Expectations* had looked back at *David Copperfield*, and various resemblances link the two Yeats works. *The Speckled Bird* has at its centre a young man who bears certain affinities to Yeats. This young man has a relationship with a girl or woman called Margaret, who resembles her namesake in *John Sherman* in being lively and beautiful (though she is also much more substantial, emotionally and intellectually, than her predecessor). Yeats probably took the name Margaret directly from the character in *John Sherman*. The protagonist of *The Speckled Bird* lives with a single parent, now his father rather than his mother; and in both novels, the second parent seems to have been removed in order to focus more attention on a single parent-child relationship. This concentration is also enhanced in both novels by the protagonist's lack of siblings.

The images of the chimera and the fruitless pursuit, prominent in *John Sherman*, reappear at the beginning of *The Speckled Bird* in Michael's quest for the pot of gold about which he has dreamed (*SB* 2). In the 'De Burgh' text Margaret tells Michael 'I was very young when we met and I had never seen anybody like you. I was dazzled by your beautiful ideas, but as I grew older I saw that they were not right, that they were against the preordained order of the world and that your whole life would be a following of chimeras and dreams' (*SB* 183–4). The nature of the chimera has changed, however: in *John Sherman* it appeared as a quest for the wrong partner or the wrong way of life, an evasion of responsibility, while in *The Speckled Bird* it is an acceptance or a pursuit of certain values in the (unpopular) belief that they are realities.

Perhaps because he never brought *The Speckled Bird* to publication standard, Yeats devotes less energy than in *John Sherman* to depicting a protagonist distinct from himself (or, it may be more accurate to say, the resemblance between author and character may have seemed too close to allow him to publish; and this hypothesis seems particularly plausible because it is his less active, less attractive side which appears in the character). Yet significant differences do remain between Yeats and Michael. While Yeats's mother apparently influenced his development less than his father did, the complete removal of the mother in *The Speckled Bird* remains a striking change from actuality. Yeats's mother died in 1900 while he was at work on the novel, but Michael is portrayed as a much younger person than Yeats at the time of writing (whereas the protagonist of *John Sherman* is older than Yeats was at the time he wrote that novel); and Michael shows no sign of remembering his mother. Michael's lack of siblings distinguishes him from Yeats; though we might reflect that Yeats's siblings are largely absent from *Autobiographies* as well. The relationship between father and son in the novel is often distant, whereas Yeats's relationship with his father was close, if sometimes antagonistic. The effect of these emphases, of course, is to stress Michael's solitude, his position as an alien character, a speckled bird.

Another striking transformation of fact appears in Michael's Catholic background. While his Catholicism never dominates his life, it sets him apart from Yeats—partly by giving him different tastes in art, as seen in his affection for Stephen

Löchner's 'Madonna in the Rose Garden'. Yeats may also have made Michael a Catholic to emphasise his loneliness as a visionary, since the Church emphatically disapproves of self-interpreted mystical experiences of the kind Michael undergoes. This disapproval adds tension to what might otherwise seem a wholly solipsistic drama. Yeats explores Catholic images in a number of his early works, but his decision to depict an autobiographical protagonist as a Catholic still seems a remarkable experiment.

Nonetheless, Michael remains in many ways close to Yeats's own position. 'Michael' is a name which Yeats liked, as he showed by bestowing it on another important and partly autobiographical character, Michael Robartes, and later on his own son. (Through the archangel Michael, the name also suggests vision and power, qualities which Yeats no doubt wished to attribute to himself.)

John, the father in *The Speckled Bird*, probably takes his name from Yeats's father.[7] In the later versions of the novel, especially the 'De Burgh' version, the father sometimes appears as a gruff, amiable, opinionated, talented but rather self-defeating artist, closely recalling our usual impression of John Butler Yeats. John Hearne's views on education, expressed in the 'Final' version, resemble those of J. B. Yeats, as O'Donnell has pointed out (*SB* 9). In the 'Island' and 'Leroy' texts, by contrast, the father has a religious intensity and a visionary quality entirely foreign to Yeats's father; these versions are too brief and tentative to show clearly what Yeats had in mind when he wrote these sketches. He may have used a different model for the father's character in these versions, and a likely one is his uncle George Pollexfen. It may also be that in these earlier versions Yeats sought to portray a parent totally unlike his own father, perhaps a man who could have been a precursor to himself rather than one whose views he felt obliged to repudiate, a visionary rather than a practical man, and a father who would allow him complete control of his own life. Michael's mother's background in these earlier versions is aristocratic, and so introduces another attempt by Yeats to create a more apparently suitable past than his real one. In the later, more realistic versions of the novel we hear that Michael's mother had been a peasant, and thus closer to the social background of Yeats's mother (who was middle-class but liked a simple, 'folk' existence) than the earlier, more aristocratic figure had been.

Yeats had difficulty evaluating his relationship with his father, as *Autobiographies* shows. This difficulty may explain why Sherman's father never appeared in Yeats's earlier novel, an absence which may, in turn, have made that novel easier for Yeats to complete. One of the reasons for Yeats's persistent difficulty in completing *The Speckled Bird* may be his decision to include the father as a character. Yeats seems to exaggerate his sense of grievance at his father's effect on his life, perhaps in an effort to exorcise such feelings: 'His father's thoughts and words filled the world for him, and to disobey his father was like disobeying God; every thought he had, almost every feeling he had, was but a shadow of some thought or of some feeling of his father's' (*SB* 120).

However, the relationship with his father is not the only, the most important or the most intimate area of Yeats's life to be considered in *The Speckled Bird*. More central are his relationships with women, and his involvement with mystical beliefs and societies—two areas which Yeats was to find it hard to treat in *Autobiographies*.

Though the Margaret of *The Speckled Bird* does resemble superficially the one in *John Sherman*, she has clearly assimilated some qualities from Maud Gonne, whom Yeats had met shortly after he completed the earlier novel. Apple blossoms glimmer above this Margaret's head (*SB* 50, 184), and Yeats frequently associated this image with Maud Gonne (see, for example, *The Trembling of the Veil*, *A* 123). Yeats also associates Margaret with Helen of Troy, as he had associated Maud Gonne (*SB* 205). Margaret refuses Michael's proposal as Maud Gonne had refused Yeats's, and in similar terms, suggesting that an ideal, Platonic and mystical relationship could be substituted for the sexual or marital relationship she will not permit. Margaret's unhappy marriage, so important in the 'Final' version, probably owes something to Maud Gonne's relationship with Lucien Millevoye, about which Yeats first heard while he was working on the novel. The apparent association with Maud Gonne's marriage to John MacBride in 1903 is probably a matter of coincidence; it seems unlikely that

Yeats worked on *The Speckled Bird* after that date.[8] Michael's response to the news of Margaret's marriage recalls Yeats's efforts in the 1890s to impress Maud Gonne and to dedicate all his labours to her: 'Oh, why did she marry? I was doing everything for her, you cannot think what a great work I have been doing here, and it was all for her I was doing it. I thought she would come back to our ideas in the end, the ideas that she used to have as much as I' (*SB* 84).

Margaret bears the name 'Olive' in a short section of the *Speckled Bird* manuscript. An association with Olivia Shakespear suggests itself, not that Yeats ever acknowledged the details of her role in his life publicly—even in his 'private' account, now in *Memoirs*, she appears as 'Diana Vernon'. Possibly he intended to create a composite portrait in the novel but failed to complete it. Part of Olivia Shakespear's role in his own life—as a mistress who consoled him when he was rejected by his beloved—is bestowed in *The Speckled Bird* upon Harriet St. George: 'This woman seemed so friendly and unexacting that he thought she would understand and demand nothing that he could not give. . . . Gradually they became closer and closer to one another, and after a time she became his mistress. This went on for two or three years, then they began to gradually drift apart. She began to seem unhappy, and he found it more and more difficult to reconcile this new relationship with the old unaltered feeling' (*SB* 105). Yeats also wrote in a note that Michael's 'discussion with Harriet would strike a note of friendship, would bring out the extreme relief with which a man very much in love escapes from the tension at times of conversation with the woman he loves by talking about her to a friend' (*SB* 230).

The Speckled Bird gives no hint of Maud Gonne's political activities, which (Yeats sometimes believed, or claimed to believe) accounted for her refusal of his proposals. This artistic transformation may be an attempt to cope with the rejection by displacing it; on the other hand, it may show an uncharacteristic acknowledgment by Yeats that even without the political activities her acceptance of him would have been unlikely.

Yeats's interest in mysticism appears in the novel still more clearly. He found it difficult to discuss this interest publicly—or with his father—and he remained dissatisfied with many of his mystical experiments. These difficulties may provide a further explanation for his inability to complete the novel. *The Speckled Bird* acknowledges such interests more fully and directly than any of his published writings; similar acknowledgment appears elsewhere only in private letters. In 1892 he wrote to John O'Leary 'Now as to Magic. It is surely absurd to hold me "weak" or otherwise because I chose to persist in a study which I decided deliberately four or five years ago to make, next to my poetry, the most important pursuit of my life. . . . The mystical life is the centre of all that I do and all that I think and all that I write' (*L* 210–11). Yeats also wrote, in a passage since published in *Memoirs*, that 'an obsession more constant than anything but my love itself was the need of mystical rites—a ritual system of evocation and meditation—to reunite the perception of the spirit, of the divine, with natural beauty' (*M* 123). Yeats hints here at the close connection between his interest in the occult and his interest in Maud Gonne, a connection which is also implied in a letter largely about Maud Gonne which he wrote to George Russell in 1891: 'Go and see her when she gets to Dublin and keep her from forgetting me and occultism' (*L* 183). O'Donnell remarks that 'Yeats was in Paris by at least 7 December 1896, ostensibly doing research for the novel, but more probably courting Maud Gonne and working on the Celtic Mysteries with MacGregor and Moina Mathers' (*SB* xl). But such activities, of course, did constitute 'research for the novel', since these related fascinations appear there as a part of Michael's life. Michael, like Yeats, wishes to impress his beloved with his esoteric knowledge and to show his superiority to others (ironically, Michael is distressed by the commonplace nature of his fellow-mystics, as Maud Gonne had been in reality). Mysticism is also an area which he can inhabit with his beloved, since she has ruled out a more intimate relationship.

Michael's interest in the occult, like Yeats's, has intrinsic importance apart from its connection to his romantic life. From the beginning, *The Speckled Bird* shows Michael's dissatisfaction with the immediate and everyday, his wish to escape to a purer world. He rejects his father's argument that 'when one has learned to live in the present, in the present scene and the present time, life has nothing more to teach one' (*SB* 7). John

Hearne's injunction here is undermined by the emphasis which the narrator places on his solitude (*SB* 6), and this contrast seems to represent a deliberate irony rather than simply a failure by Yeats to revise the passage. We are led to sympathise with Michael's lonely integrity (proved by his fasting), his belief in his own visions, his wish to find an environment where such visions might be seen as realities, and perhaps also his disappointment at the shortcomings of the various sects where this realisation at first seemed to him possible (even though we might not have shared his initial optimism about the potential success of these sects). These often shoddy groups act as foils to Michael's own thoughts, making such thoughts richer and stronger than they would otherwise be.

Yeats no doubt hoped that the relationship between his literary and his mystical interests would be harmonious. Yet a potential tension always existed, and it appears in *The Speckled Bird* as well. Maclagan writes to Michael 'I have come to recognize that you are not a magician, but some kind of an artist, and that the *summum bonum* itself, the potable gold of our masters, were less to you than some charm of colour, or some charm of words' (*SB* 92). In fact, as O'Donnell has pointed out, it seems that in *The Speckled Bird* the balance is tilted in favour of mysticism, an emphasis which would be reversed in Yeats's later work.[9] But the novel does show him earnestly considering the dilemma.

The Speckled Bird was Yeats's final attempt to embody his experiences in an extended, explicitly fictional form. Later, perhaps acknowledging the difficulty which novel-writing caused him, he wrote autobiographical fiction only in oblique and fragmentary instalments, and these fragments attached themselves like charged particles to his poems (and, eventually, to *A Vision*) rather than striving for independent life. Some of these texts were written even earlier than *The Speckled Bird* itself. The characters Michael Robartes and Owen Aherne appear together in most of these texts, and their names seem, intriguingly, to divide Michael Hearne's name into two separate entities, as if they represent a duality which Yeats also enacted within Michael Hearne himself.

Yeats found Robartes and Aherne of use for a considerable time; 'Rosa Alchemica', the first story to include either of them,

appeared in 1897 and the revised *A Vision*, where they make
their final appearance, in 1937. Indeed, Yeats had to revive
Robartes, or allow him to insist on his return, after over-hastily
killing him off. Robartes provides Yeats with access to an
experience and a viewpoint outside his own personality from
which his own situation can nevertheless be studied. Like the
curtain in *The Only Jealousy of Emer*, he allows Yeats to 'change
his mask unseen' (*CPL* 286)—from observer to observed. He
permits Yeats to become a character in his own fiction, written
about by others; and he allows us to share (with amusement, a
response Yeats seldom sought from his readers) in Yeats's
experiment in approaching the self from so strange an angle.

Since Robartes usually acts as an alien and mysterious figure
rather than (like Yeats's novel characters) a complementary
and tangible one, he tends to remain relatively undefined,
hovering on the perimeters of consciousness. Most vividly
realised as an individual in 'Rosa Alchemica', where he has
considerable presence and acts rapidly and decisively, if mys-
teriously, he later suffers progressive attenuation. Curiously,
his gradual removal from the action of the 'Rosa Alchemica'
stories corresponds to that of the narrator, who acts in the first,
speaks occasionally in the second, and merely listens in the
third. After *Michael Robartes and the Dancer*, Robartes disappears
altogether until revived for the first *A Vision*, where he expresses
gratitude to Yeats for having spread 'rumours' of his death,
since these rumours have kept the world from pursuing him.
Aherne, by contrast, resents Yeats's high-handed treatment:
'Mr Yeats had given the name of Michael Robartes and that of
Owen Aherne to fictitious characters, and made those characters live through events that were a travesty of real events'
(*1AV* xvi). The slightly farcical tone of this latter remark
heralds Robartes' final appearance, within the revised *A Vision*,
in one of Yeats's wittiest pieces of writing, 'Stories of Michael
Robartes and His Friends'. In this text Yeats demonstrates his
ability to escape the generally straightfaced presentation of
Robartes and Aherne which he had employed previously, and
to deactivate a device which had become problematic by
immersing it in comedy.

Thus Robartes and Aherne serve changing needs. Usually
they provide a means of access to arcane knowledge, permitting

Yeats to vary his attitude to such knowledge from enthusiasm through detached contemplation to scepticism and mockery (a more flexible response than the rigid structure of *The Speckled Bird* had allowed him). Because Robartes and Aherne, for all their mysterious nature, appear in close relation to the circumstances of Yeats's life, even when those circumstances are superficially altered as in 'Rosa Alchemica', sources have been sought for them in people known to Yeats. Lady Gregory thought that George Russell was a model for Robartes. Warwick Gould suggests that both Lionel Johnson and John O'Leary contributed something to Aherne, as MacGregor Mathers did to Robartes.[10] Most interesting here is an association with *Autobiographies*, which suggests more interplay between the 'factual' and 'fictional' accounts than might have been expected. The period when Robartes and Aherne disappear from Yeats's work corresponds remarkably with the period when Yeats was writing *The Trembling of the Veil*, in which he discusses in detail Lionel Johnson and his other associates of the 1890s. As Gould notes, at this stage 'Johnson assumes his own place, gathered "into the artifice" of the phantasmagoria, under his own name, and the name Aherne acquires an independent significance'.[11] After Yeats had recorded his impressions of Johnson and Mathers, Robartes and Aherne could safely return armed with doctrine derived not from associates but from Yeats's own speculations, Mrs Yeats acting, in some way, as a mediator. Thus the fictional claim that Yeats's philosophical 'System' had mystical external sources could be fitted neatly into an existing (if temporarily inactive) structure, one whose guiding assumption had always been the possibility of attaining such knowledge. The relationship of the System to Yeats's previous work thus displays that kind of reciprocity he sought throughout his writing.

In the 'Rosa Alchemica' stories, the narrator remains at a playful distance from Yeats, as if toying with his resemblances to his creator. In the first paragraph of the first story, a correspondence between poet and speaker is momentarily permitted, then progressively—and wittily—undercut. The narrator's 'cry of measureless desire for a world made wholly of essences' (*MY* 267) would have been uttered only briefly and secretly, if at all, by Yeats himself, but this desire was one he had felt privately in his earlier years. Tendencies of Yeats's own nature appear as the narrator mentions 'my mind, for which symbolism was a necessity' (*MY* 269) and remarks that 'even in my most perfect moment I would be two selves, the one watching with heavy eyes the other's moment of content' (*MY* 269). The latter remark is a revealing comment on Yeats's mind as well as an accurate appraisal of the mechanics of autobiographical writing. Yet the narrator's question, asked of Robartes, 'why should I go to Eleusis and not to Calvary?' (*MY* 274), is perhaps one asked of Yeats rather than by him; an affinity between Yeats and Robartes may be suggested here. Thus, even as Robartes serves different functions at different times, so does the narrator within this story and within the sequence of stories. Perhaps he represents that aspect of Yeats which was evoked by the prototypes of Robartes and Aherne; certainly the tones of 'Rosa Alchemica' and 'The Tables of the Law' respectively resemble, to a striking degree, Yeats's accounts in *Autobiographies* of his first meetings with Mathers and Johnson (*A* 182–8, 221–4).

Such near-identifications of poet and persona attract parody in 'Stories of Michael Robartes and His Friends', where Daniel O'Leary sounds, at times, suspiciously like Yeats, particularly when he remarks that 'my great interest is the speaking of verse, and the establishment some day or other of a small theatre for plays in verse' (*2AV* 33). Those who suspect Yeats of taking himself too seriously should ponder the implications of his allowing such a speaker some of his most cherished thoughts. O'Leary observes that the 'realists turn our words into gravel, but the musicians and the singers turn them into honey and oil', which sounds like Yeats, then adds with delightful blandness 'I have always had the idea that some day a musician would do me an injury' (*2AV* 34). Michael Robartes, introduced into the story with all due fanfare, looks like a cross between Yeats and the Ancient Mariner: 'lank, brown, muscular, clean-shaven, with an alert, ironical eye' (*2AV* 37). Robartes and Aherne echo Sherlock Holmes and Watson: '"Aherne, the book", said Robartes' (*2AV* 37); Michael J. Sidnell calls them 'a couple of spiritual detectives better informed and a move ahead of the official keepers of the conscience of mankind'.[12] These humbler beings reflect that new detachment from his material which

Yeats achieved towards the end of his life, as well as providing a comic prelude to the portentous, massively serious text—*A Vision*—which they introduce.

Yeats's diverse autobiographical fiction thus aspires towards lightness of touch, a quality best achieved in *John Sherman* and the later Michael Robartes material. The unpublished *Speckled Bird*, by contrast, remains sombre and often turgid, and one doubts that he ever could have brought it to publishable form. It may be that Yeats attempted too direct a self-depiction in this work, and consequently trapped himself in uncertainty and equivocation. Comedy and irony seem necessary for Yeats to achieve detachment in writing prose texts about his own past. They may be attained readily within the formal structure of a declared autobiography, where they have something solid (the reality of the past) against which to react, but prove more elusive in fiction.

Even if we overlook *The Speckled Bird*, however, Yeats's autobiographical fiction remains slight, especially by comparison with his poetry and drama. Ultimately far more successful as a means of self-depiction, and more appealing to readers, is his declared and ostensibly 'factual' account, *Autobiographies*.

THREE

Reveries over Childhood and Youth

Reveries over Childhood and Youth, Yeats's first sustained piece of declared autobiographical writing in prose, appears loosely constructed, a leisurely stroll through randomly selected memories. The title suggests the daydreaming of the present autobiographer, and records his wish for structural flexibility, as much as his commitment to narrate his past in detail. But the apparent artlessness of the writing in *Reveries* actually results from Yeats's commitment to technique: he laboured to make the book seem seductively spontaneous, to encourage his readers to settle comfortably into the text. Like Yeats's earlier prose works, in which he had cultivated formal qualities which he later applied skilfully in his autobiographical writings, *Reveries* is in fact highly wrought and carefully organised, its method precisely attuned to its meaning, and while the impression of 'reveries' may suit the phase of his life about which he is writing, it is inadequate for his present rhetorical purposes.

Particular views of the workings of memory bring Yeats to a particular view of structure, which helps in turn to determine the arrangement of recalled experiences within the text. Yeats may also have been encouraged or influenced by reading parts of Joyce's *A Portrait of the Artist as a Young Man* in 1914. His *Reveries* depicts another artist as a young man, and both works exploit changing styles to dramatise mimetically a developing consciousness. The impersonal, episodic manner of Yeats's first few pages recalls the opening of the *Portrait*; present tense forms and simple syntax evoke the child's responses to the world as do similar features in Joyce's novel. For both authors, fragmented and impressionistic narrative provides a means of editing experience into manageable divisions.

Further resemblances link the two works. *Reveries* depicts

Yeats from very early memories to the point where, he says boldly at the beginning of one section of text, 'I had published my first book of poems' (*A* 105); similarly, the *Portrait* takes Stephen from early memories to the villanelle and the aesthetic theory, the point where it seems possible for him to become an artist. In each case, the terminal point is reached when the protagonist acquires the ability to write books like the one in which he is currently appearing to us (*Reveries*, the *Portrait*). *Reveries* ends with the deaths of Yeats's dominating grandparents, and with a sense of release and expansiveness, which the sombre final section mutes but does not destroy. The *Portrait* ends with Stephen's symbolic escape from family, church and country. In both cases, potential artistic independence appears asserted and partially fulfilled.[1] Both books generated sequels (*The Trembling of the Veil* and *Ulysses*) in which the further fortunes of the autobiographical protagonist are treated, but where other people have become more dominant, where the central position of the protagonist is challenged from several directions simultaneously.

Yeats also gives *Reveries* structure through his manner of presenting his characters. Like many other declared autobiographers, and like Joyce in the *Portrait*, he pares away the circumstances surrounding the protagonist. His mother is scarcely mentioned, for example, and his father's role seems attenuated, in a pattern of reduction which recalls *John Sherman* and *The Speckled Bird*. Most friends and relations have their being only in the shady perimeters of the book, particularly in its later stages. Yeats substantiates this tendency to isolate the self from the world by explaining one of his modes of perception: 'I notice that now, for the first time, what I saw when alone is more vivid in my memory than what I did or saw in company' (*A* 63). Many 'formative' experiences do presumably occur to isolated individuals, keenly aware of their own solitude, and it is in isolation that one's responsibility for analysing experiences is greatest. Yeats's text seems more honest and insistent than many in its acknowledgment of these facts.

Yeats observes towards the end of *Reveries*, at the end of a section and therefore emphatically, that when he was younger 'I had as many ideas as I have now, only I did not know how to

choose from among them those that belonged to my life' (*A* 83).
The problem of creating an intellectually coherent self had
afflicted him in the past, and the same quest for authenticity
which he had undertaken in his youth demands that the
problem must be re-enacted in an account of that past, in a
form of involution common in declared autobiographical texts.
Reveries, like *Autobiographies* on a larger scale, treats Yeats's
attempts to wrestle from a resolutely plural self a satisfactorily
comprehensive 'unity of being'. In order to comprehend the
present self, it may be necessary to rediscover a succession of
past selves, such as those of childhood and youth. Yeats
remarks of his father that 'I saw his mind in fragments, which
had always hidden connections I only now begin to discover'
(*A* 66). Yeats professes to provide the hidden connections
which would make his own life seem more coherent to others
than his father's life had seemed to him, but he includes in the
text, as a kind of safety valve, his doubts about the feasibility of
the enterprise.

Despite this prominence of the autobiographical protagonist, *Reveries* also gains balance and structure from Yeats's
handling of his other characters. Yeats's grandfather William
Pollexfen dominates the first two sections of the book as a
wealthy, powerful man, and dies at the end of the book. On the
way we see him in retirement, in much reduced circumstances
(*A* 67) and consulting a doctor (*A* 85). Thus the grandfather,
and his wisdom, influence and panache, seem to decline steadily and measurably through *Reveries*, as Yeats's own qualities
develop and expand. Old William Pollexfen's extreme
reticence also marks him as a foil to the newly expansive
William Yeats, writer of *Reveries*, so making the book seem more
complete an account than we might otherwise think it.
Towards the end of the book John O'Leary appears as if to take
the place of William Pollexfen, whom he rather resembles in his
quietness and dedication to action, though he differs in his
gentleness and breadth of vision. As Yeats reaches maturity he
substitutes for a genealogically determined and often oppressive precursor a freely chosen and more liberating one (as, at
the end of the *Portrait*, Stephen Dedalus turns from his biologi-
cal father Simon to the mythical father Daedalus). At the
beginning of *Reveries* Yeats attempts to control his grandfather's

influence by transferring him from life to literature: 'Even to-day when I read *King Lear* his image is always before me, and I often wonder if the delight in passionate men in my plays and in my poetry is more than his memory' (*A* 9). Yeats recalls that at the time of his grandfather's death he published his first book of poems—a sign of artistic emancipation from his forebears.

The personalities of Yeats's grandfather and a great-grandfather (John Yeats) are contrasted through the association of each with keys. The autocratic grandfather insists that his servants should be locked inside every night and the key brought to him; but in fact 'for all the ceremonious bringing of the key the gate was never locked' (*A* 9), and the key thus represents his unsuccessful attempt to assert his authority over the servants. Yeats's great-grandfather, by contrast, always rattles his keys before entering his kitchen, 'so much did he fear finding some one doing wrong' (*A* 22). In his case, the keys show his recognition that the servants have lives of their own, and thus a successful attempt to avoid asserting authority. This contrast shows Yeats deploying a form of symbolism which he had cultivated in *The Speckled Bird* and, especially, in *John Sherman*.

Still more striking is Yeats's presentation of his father, whose increasing then declining influence on Yeats forms the basic structural pattern of *Reveries*, reinforced by much imagery of rising and falling. Near the midpoint of the book, in the fifteenth of the thirty-three sections of text, Yeats records that 'my father's influence upon my thoughts was at its height' (*A* 64). (A close verbal echo of a passage which appeared a few pages before, 'The land war was now at its height' [*A* 55], may subtly accentuate the hint of conflict between father and son.) This fifteenth section, where the father's influence is said to be strongest, immediately follows a section describing Yeats's sexual awakening, after which he will be able to supplant his father as a progenitor. It precedes a section in which Yeats describes his composition of his first poems, an assertion of artistic independence from his father, the painter (though he does begin writing in the poetic genre his father prefers, dramatic poetry). Thus while the precise historical moment of the father's greatest influence is not specified—an entirely typical omission in the virtually dateless *Reveries*—Yeats does show the central place of this moment in the sequence of his experiences or memories. Yet, paradoxically, it is the Yeats composing *Reveries* who chooses to place the moment; and the placing is skilful, dramatising neatly Yeats's growing independence throughout the phase of his life depicted in the second half of his book. An incident Yeats recalls in which his father threw a book at Yeats's head is neatly symbolic in itself, but also implies that Yeats's writing of *Reveries* has a therapeutic and retaliatory function.

The next few sections, in which his father never directly appears, show Yeats successively engaged in writing, falling secretly in love (with Laura Armstrong) and exploring the supernatural—assertions of rebellion, maturity, or difference from his father. When his father does reappear in the text it is to disagree with Yeats about Edward Dowden, mysticism, 'personal utterance' and the value of poetry; Yeats's views on these subjects now receive support from the tone and content of the text of *Reveries*, and his father's influence thus appears in steady decline. The act of writing *Reveries* is itself a further gesture of control and independence. None of this is to imply strong antagonism between father and son—though *First Draft* reveals that such antagonism sometimes became intense—but rather shows a conscious decision by Yeats to organise his *Reveries* around his father's role in his life, to weigh his own growing independence precisely against his father's declining power.

Yeats's treatment of many of his minor figures involves a careful delineation of contrasts between a character and himself; such a technique becomes especially prominent in the account of John F. Taylor: 'I braved Taylor again and again as one might a savage animal as a test of courage, but always found him worse than my expectation' (*A* 97). This manner of presentation emphasises Yeats's sense of his difference from others, hence his uniqueness and his isolation. The presentation of Taylor here, as antithetical to Yeats in a symbolic manner as well as in particular circumstances, anticipates the treatment of George Moore in *Dramatis Personae*.

Yeats's treatment of some of his minor characters may seem partial—in both senses of the word, 'biased' and 'incomplete'—but he quite properly concerns himself chiefly with his efforts to define himself in contrast with those around him. The published partial treatments of himself by Katharine Tynan, George Moore and others must also have encouraged him to work in this way.

Yeats's division of his text into short sections is another device which helps him to control continuity and pace, as well as implying that he wishes to depict his experiences in a series of incidents or anecdotes rather than claiming for them more continuity than they had in fact possessed. Changes in his life are also conveyed structurally by such means. A typical early section leads directly to its successor in mood and often in setting. The later sections depart abruptly in new directions, following a pattern which suggests the increasingly varied and volitional quality of Yeats's interests as he matured, and parallels his deliberate, energetic exploration of various possible courses of behaviour and choices of allegiance. Later sections, moreover, are consistently shorter than earlier ones. Of the first seventeen sections (about half the total number) only two occupy less than one page in the 1955 text, while in the remainder of the book six sections are less than one page in length and three more are only slightly longer. The midpoint of the text in terms of page distribution occurs in the tenth of the thirty-three sections; thus the later sections average only half the length of the earlier ones. The effect of this reduction in section-length is to increase the apparent speed of the text, and this quickening tempo mimics Yeats's transition from the static scenes of childhood to the rapid changes of his adolescence and the busy pace of his early adult life. We thus have a sense of his increasing energy and autonomy, reinforced by a subtle use of literary structure.

A further organising device which Yeats uses in *Reveries* is the manipulation of time. At first it seems that his insistent specification of place accords with (and perhaps justifies) a vagueness about time, as though his reveries will follow the ebb and flow of visual recollections but neglect historical order. The insistent use of present tense forms early in *Reveries*, and the common use of the passive voice throughout, create an impression of timelessness, and Yeats also avoids specific allusions to dates and to historical sequences. Marjorie Perloff implicitly attacks Yeats for producing in *Reveries* a disconcerting 'temporal displacement'.[2] Yet Yeats's technique here is conscious, consistent, purposive and appropriate. He persistently avoids mentioning particular dates because he wishes to create new connections among phases of his life, and thus in effect to change the shape of the life. The beginning of *The Trembling of the Veil* appears to provide a striking contrast to this manner, with its firm, precise initial section-title 'Four Years: 1887–1891' and its brisk opening phrase 'At the end of the eighties' (*A* 113). Nevertheless, Yeats remains evasive and manipulative in his treatment of time even here, and the contrast with *Reveries* remains more apparent than real. We might also recall the absurd, self-parodic specificity of time suggested in the opening lines of *John Sherman*.

Throughout *Autobiographies*, in fact, times are important in the way they interrelate in Yeats's text rather than in connection with external, 'clock' time. In 'Four Years' Yeats remarks 'I saw a good deal of Wilde at that time—was it 1887 or 1888?—I have no way of fixing the date except that I had published my first book, *The Wanderings of Oisin*, and that Wilde had not yet published his *Decay of Lying*' (*A* 134). Here, time becomes a function of the progress of one's life and especially of one's publishing life; 'truth of feeling' tends to supplant 'truth of fact'. Later in *Autobiographies*, in *Dramatis Personae*, Yeats will use a strikingly similar (though more negative) construction in describing the paintings at Coole: 'Those that I keep most in memory are a Canaletto, a Guardi, a Zurbarán. Two or three that once hung there had, before I saw those great rooms, gone to the National Gallery, and the fine portraits by Augustus John and Charles Shannon were still to come' (*A* 390). Here, the past becomes that which is removed before we enter the present; the future, that which will appear after we leave. Perloff notes that in *Autobiographies* Yeats will use a word like 'presently' to denote 'an immeasurable lapse of time';[3] but he does so in order to fuse the reader's sense of the present and his own, and to impress on others the usefulness of his own impressionistic flexibility of recollection. That he intends time to have this kind of fluidity is implied in an anecdote he recounts in which 'I heard one boy say to another it was something wrong with my liver that gave me such a dark complexion and that I could not live more than a year' (*A* 29–30), to which Yeats's response, he claims, had been the reflection that 'a year is a very long time, one can do such a lot of things in a year'.

Similarly, when Yeats opens a paragraph with the words 'I began' without indication of time, we should accept as part of his meaning that the fact of a new start, occurring at this moment to his recollecting mind, is more important than the date at which it had in actuality taken place: the time-sequence of the narrator, in other words, is more important than that of the protagonist. Yeats acknowledges here that the imaginative autobiographer should be concerned primarily with present views of the past rather than with the details of that past. Perloff claims that Yeats implicitly rejects the notion of a linear time sense, but 'rejection' seems too strong a term—in *Autobiographies* he simply has no need of such a sense. The movement of his mind which he describes in *The Trembling of the Veil*, in particular, is not the kind of linear progression measured by dates but an expansion or exfoliation, which he expresses by making the perceptions of that expanding mind itself his measure of development.

Yeats's sense of place is vivid but also impressionistic: there are no leisurely detailed descriptions, but the atmosphere of particular environments is economically evoked. Dialectical relationships are established between places, especially Sligo, London and Dublin, which recall the Sligo/London polarity in *John Sherman*. The tension between Sligo and London appears particularly strongly in the first section and the last three sections of the text; thus all of *Reveries* seems to take place in the context of this duality, mediating (as Yeats himself did) between the extremes.

Besides these broader patterns, Yeats exploits in *Reveries* his rhetorical skill in handling suggestive details and images, verbal repetitions and juxtapositions. His narrative subtlety makes these features inconspicuous, but they help unobtrusively to generate mood.

The recollections detailed on the first page, strangely described by Joseph Ronsley as composing 'an Edenic view of [Yeats's] own beginnings',[4] actually seem to represent threat, decay and alienation: in Ireland the walls are crumbling and in London Yeats is told that someone may blow up the town.[5] Yeats thus sets the scene for his account of the discontents of childhood and of his later efforts to free himself from them; from the outset he seems subjected to the productions of time. The second section of the text concerns itself chiefly with heightened, imaginative and mystical experiences of various kinds, moving bathetically from Yeats's belief in the voice of conscience to his first experience of intoxication; thus Yeats establishes a pattern of grandeur deflated which recalls Joyce's *Portrait* and anticipates Yeats's own later autobiographical writing.

The fourth section of the text (in which Yeats's father appears for the first time) includes an implicit attack on attempts to deny the reality of the physical world, a reality which may be more magical than the fanciful theories set against it: from an encyclopaedia Yeats recalls 'a long passage considering whether fossil wood despite its appearance might not be only a curiously shaped stone' (*A* 25). In the same section, Yeats's first apprehensions of sex and death appear in ominous juxtaposition (*A* 26–7). His childhood discovery of the facts of sexuality depressed him, or so he claims here (his account of the same experience in his unpublished text called *First Draft*, written soon after *Reveries*, is more expansive and shows a more intricate response). His discovery of death leaves him relatively unmoved: 'I heard feet running past and heard somebody say in the passage that my younger brother, Robert, had died. He had been ill for some days. A little later my sister and I sat at the table, very happy, drawing ships with their flags half-mast high. . . . It must have been after this that I told my grandmother I did not want to go with her when she went to see old bed-ridden people because they would soon die' (*A* 27). Yeats's recalled reaction here convincingly shows the coolness typical of a child's ignorant or confused response to death; what is striking is that he seemingly feels no need to justify these attitudes retrospectively. The child's feeling, in other words, is presented dramatically; and once again, analogies with Joyce's manner of presenting Stephen Dedalus in the *Portrait* come to mind.

Examples of this kind could be multiplied extensively throughout *Reveries*. They show a highly deliberate use of style. Yeats claims that at school he had been expected to concentrate his attention on Shakespeare's grammar, and that to him content had seemed more important than this pedantic preoccupation with form. He also remarks critically of his father that 'he no longer read me anything for its story, and all our discussion was of style' (*A* 66). Yet in his own book, meaning as well as mood is often conveyed by structural and stylistic means rather than through the semantic surface of the text. The critical reference to modes of responding to Shakespeare, and the implicit criticism of his father's aestheticism, may even aim to deflect attention from Yeats's own rhetoric to his content.

The effect of *Reveries* thus depends on Yeats's use of various devices of structure which imply spontaneity even while they reveal artful planning. He controls the appearance of his autobiographical protagonist by subordinating the circumstances of his dominant father and grandfather to the circumstances of his book. Thus he re-enacts the artistic strategies he had used in early life to assert himself against the influence of his relatives: he begins writing poetry at the time of his father's greatest power over his life, and publishes his first book at the time of his grandfather's death. These two recollections form the midpoint and the conclusion of *Reveries*. Yeats uses the sections of his text to convey a sense of the increasing pace of his development and also to show his intensifying volition and expanding inventiveness. His manipulation of time and space gives an impression of 'reveries', of recalled scenes floating through the mind, but also helps to organise his past in that sequence which best suits his purposes. Various textual details subtly determine the moods of Yeats's discourse.

Yeats ends *Reveries* with the reflection that life prepares us for what never happens. The remark might seem lugubrious and even disingenuous, given the richness of Yeats's achievements by the time he wrote *Reveries*, but similar sentiments appear elsewhere in his work, as if to confirm his repeated acceptance of this view of experience. The melancholy tone of the comment accords with the apparent mood of much of *Autobiographies*. Yet the very position of *Reveries* as a part of the finished *Autobiographies* (which of course did not yet exist when *Reveries* was written) also implies that the claim is premature. Each stage of life prepares for the next, and this fact must be a positive value for the Yeats whose horizons constantly expanded and who said he had become happier with each year of life (*Autobiog-*

raphies will end with Yeats's acceptance of the Nobel Prize, further and more public confirmation of his persistent achievement). Each stage of life also anticipates its own interpretation, an activity which is Yeats's central purpose in *Autobiographies* and in much of his other writing. The act of interpreting the past inevitably gives that past a kind of validity, and Yeats's sombre conclusion to *Reveries* is partly contradicted by *Reveries* itself. But it is contradicted still more emphatically by his perseverance in writing the remaining parts of *Autobiographies*.

FOUR

The Trembling of the Veil

The Trembling of the Veil, Yeats's finest, most elegant and most powerful prose text, also strikes many readers as one of his most perplexing. Its local and general effects often seem to diverge. Much of the diction is surprisingly down-to-earth, for example, yet the syntax tends to Paterian elegance and loftiness. Some of the individual vignettes seem impersonal or abstract, but the effect of the whole volume remains curiously warm and engaging. Although *The Trembling of the Veil* remains by most standards an excellent and memorable autobiographical account, its depictions of Yeats's associates are often diffuse or of questionable accuracy, and (more disconcertingly) it says little directly about Yeats himself.

When Yeats began to write *The Trembling of the Veil* in 1920 he had in mind both *Reveries over Childhood and Youth*, written in 1914, and his so-called *First Draft*, which he had written in 1915–17. The relationships among these three texts throw light on some of the problems posed to readers by *The Trembling of the Veil*.

'Four Years' begins by recording the Yeats family's return to Bedford Park, where they had lived at a period of Yeats's life which he had already described in *Reveries*. This device links the two books, *Reveries over Childhood and Youth* and *The Trembling of the Veil*, geographically and in terms of the pattern of Yeats's life. It also begins *The Trembling of the Veil* on a note of experience, of descent to the commonplace (house-drains are mentioned), of slightly jaded rediscovery rather than of fresh exploration. The opening of *Ulysses*, which Joyce was writing at the time Yeats wrote *The Trembling of the Veil*, and which like Yeats's text is partly a sequel to an earlier, lyrical autobiographical text, embodies a remarkably similar mood. Yeats's prevailing tone now expresses sadness: 'I remember feeling disappointed because the co-operative stores, with their little seventeenth-century panes, had lost the romance I saw there when I passed them still unfinished on my way to school' (*A* 113); the charm of an earlier age, in other words, has vanished for Yeats. He reflects 'I could not understand where the charm had gone that I had felt, when as a schoolboy of twelve or thirteen I had played among the unfinished houses, once leaving the marks of my two hands, blacked by a fall among some paint, upon a white balustrade' (*A* 114); so 'completion', experience, have taken him out of the innocent, 'white' childhood world. This poignant tone recalls the mood of both the opening and closing passages of *Reveries*, so linking *The Trembling of the Veil* both cyclically and sequentially with the earlier work. Yeats did, in fact, move several paragraphs physically out of *Reveries* at this point, as he incorporated equivalent material into *The Trembling of the Veil*.

Nevertheless, *The Trembling of the Veil* goes on to qualify the pessimism Yeats had expressed at the end of *Reveries*. While Yeats recounts disappointments, setbacks and confusions, he also acknowledges that he made much progress in the years recorded in *The Trembling of the Veil*. This progress was particularly evident in the literary and public life which *The Trembling of the Veil* treats in most detail (had he concentrated on his romantic life, for example, as he did in *The Speckled Bird*, the impression would inevitably have been considerably bleaker). The minimal expectations for the future expressed at the end of *Reveries* provide a rhetorical foil for the major achievements recounted in *The Trembling of the Veil*, and may even have been included in anticipation of such contrasts. Yeats's father, who dominated his life in the period treated in *Reveries*, scarcely appears now; the later book shows Yeats much more detached from his family, even though he did in fact live with them for most of this period.

The Trembling of the Veil further resembles *Reveries* in the kinds of use which it makes of partly autonomous sections of text. Often these sections present a succession of 'characters', each depicted in an appropriate setting. Another resemblance to *Reveries* appears in Yeats's tendency to be specific about place but non-committal about time: on one occasion he even remarks rather absurdly that 'I am certain of one date, for I have gone to much trouble to get it right' (*A* 343), as if to justify his serene but purposive neglect of specific time elsewhere in the text. A few precise verbal and imagistic echoes of *Reveries* occur: for example, Yeats's account of quarrels and thefts about the time of Verlaine's funeral (*A* 342) recalls his treatment of the similar events which marked the death of his own grandfather (*A* 106). Yeats's depiction of William Morris in *The Trembling of the Veil* also recalls the manner of representing his grandfather, and the affinities between his grandfather and John O'Leary, which he had employed in *Reveries*.

If *Reveries* resembles in some respects Joyce's *Portrait*, *The Trembling of the Veil* also demonstrates interesting resemblances to that novel, not that any of these is specific enough to demonstrate 'influence'. Yeats employs the same five-part structure which Joyce had used.[1] In both books, the first of the five parts covers the later 1880s and makes structural use of the death of Parnell (a pattern which Yeats's titles for his first two parts, 'Four Years: 1887–1891' and 'Ireland after Parnell', strongly reinforce). Again, as in *Reveries*, Yeats begins his text with a somewhat Joycean series of fragmentary recollections, though they are now more strongly linked to each other in a causal sequence, as seems appropriate to the more mature protagonist. The text moves through a process of accretion to a moment of incipient artistic fruition: *The Trembling of the Veil* ends with Yeats on the verge of establishing with Synge and Lady Gregory the Irish dramatic movement which will become a central subject of all his later autobiographical volumes, culminating in Yeats's tribute to Lady Gregory and Synge in *The Bounty of Sweden*. As in the *Portrait*, private and public concerns alternate, but again there is a general movement outwards from the individual to the social. *The Trembling of the Veil*, like the *Portrait*, depicts in its central third section a spiritual crisis undergone by the protagonist, and Yeats's third section ('Hodos Chameliontos') also recalls the third chapter of Joyce's *Portrait* in its emphasis on the oppression of the protagonist by external forces. Both *The Trembling of the Veil* and the *Portrait* also make extensive use of imagery of gestation and birth.

However, *The Trembling of the Veil* also departs from earlier patterns. Yeats no longer employs the varying lengths of sections of text for elaborate rhetorical purposes as he had done in *Reveries*, perhaps because he no longer wishes to emphasise change or differing degrees of stability: as an adult he leads a more balanced life. Occasionally, though, a particularly short section will still be used for emphasis, as in the fifth section of 'Four Years' (treating his first meeting with Maud Gonne), the sixth of nine sections of 'Hodos Chameliontos' (in which the meaning of that mysterious term is teasingly revealed for the first time, near the end of the book) and the fourteenth section of 'The Tragic Generation' (in which Yeats relates Dowson's humorous, bitter anecdote about Wilde at Dieppe). Yeats also uses the endings of sections of text to emphasise important discoveries or ideas. Frequently (nine times in *The Trembling of the Veil*, as against only one occurrence in *Reveries*) he ends a section with a rhetorical question. These questions, like those concluding many of his poems, seem to leave matters open but in fact circumscribe interpretation, sometimes because the answer is apparent and the question thus teasing, sometimes because Yeats obviously considers the answer a matter of indifference: while readers dutifully ponder, or at least pause, he escapes quietly into his next section. He also ends some sections with marvellously eloquent and unanswerable comments: 'If, as I think, minds and metals correspond, the goldsmiths of Paris foretold the French Revolution when they substituted steel for that unserviceable gold in the manufacture of the more expensive jewel work, and made those large, flat steel buttons for men of fashion wherein the card-sharpers were able to study the reflections of the cards' (*A* 231). Readers are supposed to be so charmed by Yeats's eloquence here that no question of the plausibility of the claim will cross their minds. In some such cases Yeats relies on largely 'poetic' means of convincing—deft use of rhythm, repetition and alliteration, for example—as when he says 'I . . . believe that the first flying-fish first leaped, not because it sought "adaptation" to the air, but out of horror of the sea' (*A* 143).

In many other respects *The Trembling of the Veil* advances beyond Yeats's techniques in *Reveries*, especially in its treatment of character. For example, in *Reveries* Yeats provides several views of himself, implicitly challenging his reader to help compose his persona; in *The Trembling of the Veil* Yeats seems more central, but paradoxically less visible, and appears rather through his relationships with other people. His method of depicting himself (and especially of illustrating changes in himself) through his accounts of others, developed in *Reveries*, now evolves to a new stage in which Yeats as a distinct being becomes more difficult to see. Here, however, it will be useful to glance at *First Draft*, since this text helped him to develop these new methods.[2]

In *Reveries* Yeats expressed and transcended part of his past, that part which through distance and perspective he felt to be most nearly detachable from his present self; he says in his Preface 'now that I have written it out, I may even begin to forget it all' (*A* 3). Subsequent phases of his life seemed too intricately entangled with his present state to be treated in a similarly detached fashion. He wrote to his father on 26 December 1914: 'Yesterday I finished my memoirs [*Reveries*]; I have brought them down to our return to London in 1886 or 1887. After that there would be too many living people to consider and they would have besides to be written in a different way. While I was immature I was a different person and I can stand apart and judge. Later on, I should always, I feel, write of other people. I dare say I shall return to the subject but only in fragments' (*L* 589).

Yeats's attempt to persevere with his memoirs 'in a different way' initially took the form of *First Draft*, written in 1915–17 and not at first intended for publication. He wrote to his father late in 1915 'I am going on with the book but the rest shall be for my own eye alone' (*L* 603). Possibly Yeats aimed to write a text a little too frank for publication in order to clarify the kind and degree of omissions he would need to make if he did publish: he never includes large quantities of obviously unpublishable material. He may have used a similar method when composing *Reveries*; his typescript for that volume included the suggestion that John F. Taylor was the illegitimate son of a great Dublin lawyer, an implication which, predictably, he omitted from the published text. In *First Draft*, Yeats's self-criticism never approaches the candour found in his 1909 diary, while there are frank references to his sexual awakening and his relationship with Maud Gonne—matters which seemingly required little new analysis in 1916 but an account of which he might someday publish, if in a modified form. In fact, he never did achieve such candour in public—which is not to say that he should have done so, merely to point out that he once contemplated the attempt and then changed his mind—and references to his sexuality in *Autobiographies* often seem evasive even when we allow for the demands of public propriety. Between *First Draft* and *Autobiographies* Maud Gonne's role diminishes even more strikingly than does Emma Clery's between Joyce's *Stephen Hero* and *A Portrait of the Artist as a Young Man*; and for both Yeats and Joyce, one purpose of these particular changes is to emphasise the solitude of the autobiographical protagonist.

First Draft sounds already quite polished and poised, though it preserves the ragged edges of everyday life more fully than does its successor *The Trembling of the Veil*. As Denis Donoghue points out, the gap in time between the events described and the composition of the text helped to ensure this kind of detached assessment: 'the Autobiography required not merely an act of memory on Yeats's part, but an approach to the meaning of the lives it recited, not least his own' (*M* 9). Already Yeats considers particular lives as representative, and tries to fit them into a pattern. Most of the characters treated in *First Draft* appear again in *The Trembling of the Veil*, though a few people and scenes were saved, in revision, to appear first in *Dramatis Personae*. Even though Yeats did not always draw directly on *First Draft* when writing *The Trembling of the Veil*, it is easy to see how it functioned as a site for experiments whose results were carried over into the later work.

In its sophistication and complexity, then, *The Trembling of the Veil* owes something to its forebears *Reveries* and *First Draft*. Some of the apparent textual contradictions in *The Trembling of the Veil* may result from the differing, occasionally clashing, colours of its bibliographical tributaries.

Nevertheless *The Trembling of the Veil*, especially in its earlier divisions, shows evidence of detailed planning. It was more heavily revised than other parts of *Autobiographies* (except for *Estrangement* and *The Death of Synge*, which required extensive reworking because they had begun life as diary entries, and where the revision therefore takes a completely different form).

Its literary effects, even when puzzling, result from authorial intention as well as from the process of textual evolution.

Thus Yeats both enhances local effects and unifies the whole text by using emblematic attributes to reinforce his depiction of characters. We remember Jack Nettleship's enormous cocoa-cup (*A* 156) and Lionel Johnson's secluded, monastic study with its heavy curtains (*A* 304–5). Some of the less successful artists are seen as static and mechanical like the objects associated with them. One painter appears among his toy trains and soldiers, which trivialise life in the same way that, Yeats implies, his art does (*A* 118–19). His 'Thames barge [which] hung from the ceiling' seems a particularly apt emblem of futility and stasis, especially when juxtaposed with Yeats's observation that all the failed artists of the 1890s were 'a little like becalmed ships'; we might also contrast it with the (more useful) bookshelves which Johnson wanted hung from the ceiling (*A* 304–5). Florence Farr, at a moment when Yeats feels mildly antagonistic towards her, is associated with a sterile childhood game played with pieces of bone (*A* 122). Yeats presents Maud Gonne in a similarly emblematic but calcu-latedly ambivalent manner, so evoking a self-defeating aspect of her kind of strength: her caged birds represent vitality but also entrapment, are grand and striking as natural objects but trivial and pretentious as possessions.

In *The Trembling of the Veil*, as occasionally elsewhere in *Autobiographies*, Yeats deploys other characters to depict aspects of his own personality. His recognition of a particular quality in another person, his method here implies, demonstrates its existence in himself. Thus George Russell represents Yeats's visionary quality, Synge his integrity, Lady Gregory his gra-ciousness; as he says in *Estrangement*, almost certainly with himself and Lady Gregory in mind, 'a great lady is as simple as a good poet' (*A* 462). Yeats caused Lady Gregory and Synge to represent or enhance aspects of himself in real life as well: specifically, his interest in Irish folklore and folk theatre became embodied in them in a manner of which Yeats seems to have been wholly conscious. That he saw them, in some measure, as aspects or extensions of himself will be implied again in his remark in his Stockholm lecture, 'a young man's ghost should have stood upon one side of me and at the other a living woman sinking into the infirmity of age' (*A* 571). Daniel T. O'Hara has alluded to this method of characterisation, even suggesting that Yeats uses George Moore as an embodiment of Yeats's own 'natural' self.[3] (Yeats would, no doubt, have denied that he was using such a technique in Moore's case, and he does contrast Moore's character explicitly with his own; but O'Hara's suggestion remains provocative.) This method of characterisation is a gesture of control which seems to keep the reality of other people at a distance, and so it contributes to that aloofness which many readers feel in *Autobiographies*. At the same time, it shows Yeats's keen awareness of the nature of the relationships between himself and others, thus infusing a kind of intimacy. It allows him that blend of involvement and detachment he found necessary when dealing both with other people and with his own past. If he felt that he was no longer a 'different person' (different, that is, from his present self) in the phase of life treated in *The Trembling of the Veil*, as he had been in that treated in *Reveries*, he could still achieve objectivity, depict himself as if he really were a different person, by evoking his own character through his portraits of others.

Yeats's curiously elusive mode of characterisation serves a further purpose. *The Trembling of the Veil*, his most polished prose autobiography, is also his most 'thematic'. Its central theme has links with Yeats's mystical experiments, with *Per Amica Silentia Lunae* and with *A Vision*: this is Yeats's belief that an artist achieves full self-expression only by embracing the Anti-self, by seeking to become a different being, by acting out the drama of the self's own conflicting characteristics. This theme is expressed more clearly later in *Autobiographies*. In *Estrangement*, for example, Yeats writes: 'If we cannot imagine ourselves as different from what we are and assume that second self, we cannot impose a discipline upon ourselves, though we may accept one from others. Active virtue as distinguished from the passive acceptance of a current code is therefore theatrical, consciously dramatic, the wearing of a mask. It is the condition of arduous full life. One constantly notices in very active natures a tendency to pose, or if the pose has become a second self a preoccupation with the effect they are producing' (*A* 469). In *The Death of Synge* he adds 'I think that all happiness depends on the energy to assume the mask of some other self;

that all joyous or creative life is a rebirth as something not oneself, something which has no memory and is created in a moment and perpetually renewed' (*A* 503). Yeats never makes such points so explicitly in *The Trembling of the Veil*; such reticence has, of course, its own rhetorical appropriateness.

The characters whom Yeats treats most fully in *The Trembling of the Veil* are not necessarily the most admirable or the most influential people, or those to whom Yeats had been closest, but those who best illustrate this philosophical theme. The clearest such example must be Oscar Wilde, who exemplifies Yeats's conviction that 'we begin to live when we have conceived life as tragedy' (*A* 189). Wilde had 'turned his style to a parade as though it were his show, and he Lord Mayor' (*A* 284). Yeats hears of Wilde's action against Queensberry while staying in Sligo and about to visit 'Cochrane of the Glen'. At Cochrane's, Yeats encounters a mad girl who 'would take a flower from the vase in front of her and push it along the tablecloth towards any male guest who sat near' (*A* 284), perhaps becoming for Yeats a grotesque parody of Wilde himself, or of the world's distorted view of Wilde. Cochrane announces his conviction that 'the world is getting more manly', anticipating Yeats's pronounce- ment about Wilde 'I was certain that, guilty or not guilty, he would prove himself a man'.

Depressed by his troubles, Wilde writes 'the best short story in the world' (*A* 286) and repeats it to himself ritualistically several times a day; Yeats remarks movingly and memorably of this story 'I no more doubt its sincerity than I doubt that his parade of gloom, all that late rising and sleeping away his life, that elaborate playing with tragedy, was an attempt to escape from an emotion by its exaggeration' (*A* 287). Wilde's praise for Yeats's story 'The Crucifixion of the Outcast' indicates, Yeats implies, his identification with the character in the story, his seeking to play a part in literature, to become a mythical figure or an archetype. Wilde in his lofty sense of tragedy is juxtaposed with his brother, whom Yeats depicts as scatter- brained and immersed in contingency. Wilde's trial becomes a play or a pageant,[4] and Yeats claims at the end of his section on Wilde that 'when the verdict was announced the harlots in the street outside danced upon the pavement' (*A* 291), as if they formed a Greek chorus. In one of his shrewd, understated and provocative juxtapositions, Yeats begins his next section of text with an historical account of the attainment of 'Unity of Being', and the explanations offered by his theory of the phases of the moon; only towards the end of this section does he invoke Wilde explicitly: 'Men who belong by nature to the nights near to the full are still born, a tragic minority, and how shall they do their work when too ambitious for a private station, except as Wilde of the nineteenth Phase, as my symbolism has it, did his work?' (*A* 293).

Characters who express their true natures do so, like Wilde, by seeking to realise and become their opposites. Others fail because they cannot make this kind of effort, remaining instead confined to their existing personality or their existing relationship with the world; these include people who fail largely by Yeats's standards (Bernard Shaw) and those who fail by the world's standards as well as by Yeats's own (John Davidson). Davidson, Yeats hints, failed to search for 'perfection of thought and feeling' (*A* 315), remaining instead subject to immediate, chaotic impressions. Davidson's suspicion that the world opposes him is really an excuse for his own sense of failure, his inability to realise himself. Yeats suggests that Davidson should have modelled himself on Dowson or Johnson, men who did aspire to become their own opposites and who also possessed 'conscious deliberate craft' (*A* 318) and scholarship. Yeats's final dismissal of Davidson is compassionate but unequivocal: 'With enough passion to make a great poet, through meeting no man of culture in early life, he lacked intellectual receptivity, and, anarchic and indefinite, lacked pose and gesture, and now no verse of his clings to my memory' (*A* 318). This may seem a harsh judgment, from the author of some of the century's most memorable verse, but it accords with Yeats's insistence on the need to create one's character consciously, using other people as models or foils if necessary, rather than drifting into direct and uncritical self-expression.

Yeats wrote of 'Four Years' that 'I study every man I meet at some moment of crisis—I alone have no crisis' (*L* 675). We know from other sources that the four years in question were, in fact, a troubled time for Yeats; the phrasing of his disclaimer is unconvincing; but the text of *The Trembling of the Veil* in itself casts doubt on Yeats's remark. His fascination with the personal problems of his contemporaries discloses anxiety about his own life. Though he emerged brilliantly as a survivor in the end, there had been moments when such an outcome was far from certain, as he admits obliquely: 'I was at Sligo when I received a letter from John O'Leary, saying that I could do no more in Dublin, for even the younger men had turned against me, were "jealous", his letter said, though what they had to be jealous of God knows' (*A* 229). Yeats's refusal to explain the meaning of such hints makes the attentive reader uneasy, as he must have known it would, and this anxiety seems to mirror his own feelings.

Yeats's doctrine of the Anti-self, diligently applied to his contemporaries, also reflects his meditations on his own perso-nality, his own desire to embrace his opposite, to be (for example) a man of action as well as an artist. The denial of the 'primary self' and the recreation of the 'mask', or real self, doctrines espoused in later sections of *Autobiographies* as well as in *A Vision*, are linked with strong forces in Yeats's own character; in turn, this firm naturalistic basis for esoteric doctrines legitimates Yeats's association between the doctrines and his mode of writing in *Autobiographies* itself. That is, the relation between his present narrating self and his past recalled self resembles that between the primary self and the mask, and both relationships seem to be necessities of his questing, rest-less, creative present being. The autobiography thus rests on assumptions about personality which can be seen to develop consistently within it. *Autobiographies* is, among other things, a series of attempts to achieve unity of being despite changes in form; and in this, it obviously resembles the structure of Yeats's developing consciousness. Thus, not only does Yeats use other characters to depict himself, he also expresses through his depiction of those characters a thematic preoccupation which is centrally concerned with his own state.

Yeats's thematic focus expands to include more general meditations on the relationship of art and life (a preoccupation throughout *Autobiographies*, but especially dominant in *The Trembling of the Veil*). Usually he prefers to represent this concern as a function of his evolving character. Yet of all the elements of *Autobiographies* which seem to reflect the imposed interests of the recording autobiographer rather than the recalled preoccupations of the recorded self, such themes stand out most clearly. Yeats's belief that art could act as a compensation for difficulties in life appears in *Per Amica Silentia Lunae*, where a man's work is seen as 'flight from his entire horoscope' (*MY* 328), and such perceptions occur frequently in *Autobiographies*. Yeats sees poetry as therapy for the world (*A* 194), and suggests that mystical symbols can affect physical health, claiming to have cured his uncle George Pollexfen's fever by such means (*A* 268–9). Self-parodically, he envisages a reciprocal process when he contemplates sleeping on a board to cure himself of stylistic extravagance (*A* 371). This kind of literal embodiment of a metaphor anticipates the transformations shown, a few years later, in the second section of 'The Tower' (*CP* 219–22). A similarly ironic exploitation of the interaction of art and life appears in the description of Charles Gavan Duffy dropping a hot coal into the centre of a book 'so that nothing remained but the borders of every page' (*A* 224); life's insensitivity (or sheer clumsiness) can thus destroy a work of art. More whimsically, Yeats mentions an intrusion of art into life by painted horses reported to have trampled real ricefields (*A* 186). He suggests that this instance is more than merely whimsical by echoing his current book's title, The Trembling of the Veil, in his reference to the horses' appearance of 'trembling into stillness' (*A* 186). Thus he insists on the power of art to convey a vivid impression of reality, and quietly draws attention to the artistic dimension of *The Trembling of the Veil*.

Yeats also anticipates a concern which he later title *Dramatis Personae* will imply: an interest in the reciprocal relationship of drama and life (as Yeats's work in the theatre came to shape his life, and as his friends and contemporaries seemed to compose a dramatic scene). He faults *Arms and the Man* for representing 'logical straightness and not the crooked road of life' (*A* 283). 'The Tragic Generation' begins and ends with accounts of Yeats watching plays at the theatre, denoting structurally this recurrent preoccupation; but in the case of both the plays in question, *A Doll's House* and *Ubu Roi*, Yeats feels full of doubts. Despite his comment on *Arms and the Man*, he finds *A Doll's House* too close to mundane life to embody that heightening of everyday reality which art should achieve, and which has affinities with the doctrine of the Anti-self. He has similar reservations about *Ubu Roi*: 'Comedy, objectivity, has displayed its growing power once more' (*A* 348). The troubled relationship between drama and life is associated with the difficult personal lives of artists who lived through this time, and provides a further correlative for the failure of so many of these artists to realise themselves.

Yeats's reinforcement of his themes takes subtle forms. The wryly negative prognosis of his future life which he places at the end of *Reveries* undercuts the futile aspiration of some autobiographies to completeness, and insists that an account of one's own life must lead back, at some point, into that life. Each section of *The Trembling of the Veil* ends with a conflict between confinement and expansion, expressed literally in the content of the text and often reinforced by fragmented literary structure as well: his text struggles against inertia for open-endedness, as Yeats felt his quest for artistic freedom required a struggle against the oppressive qualities of his environment. The final section of 'Four Years' begins: 'I used to tell the few friends to whom I could speak these secret thoughts that I would make the attempt in Ireland but fail, for our civilization, its elements multiplying by division like certain low forms of life, was all-powerful; but in reality I had the wildest hopes' (*A* 194). Thus Yeats ends this part of his book by emphasising both his desire to become an Irish writer and the anxiety which this desire causes him.

'Ireland after Parnell' ends with paradox on a larger scale. The penultimate section ends with one of Yeats's unanswerable pronouncements, 'Is it not certain that the Creator yawns in earthquake and thunder and other popular displays, but toils in rounding the delicate spiral of a shell?' (*A* 249), a remark which doubtless applies to literary composition—it recalls 'Adam's Curse'—and casts a favourable light over Yeats's own methods. The final section, prepared for by this hint of textual poise and delicacy (which ensures that a markedly fragmentary structure, adopted now for the first time in *Autobiographies*, will be seen as deliberate), contains four vignettes all of which involve mysticism or orthodox religion or (especially) the clash between them. These passages evoke a social context for Yeats's mystical experiments, and anticipate the problems he treats in the next section, 'Hodos Chameliontos'. That section in turn ends with emphasis on the doctrine of the mask, the embracing of opposites, reinforced by a quotation from Yeats's poem on that subject, 'Ego Dominus Tuus'. 'The Tragic Generation' again concludes with fragments expressing various kinds of opposition, particularly the opposition between mystical belief (or experience) and the mundane world. 'The Stirring of the Bones' ends with fragmentary sections mostly concerned with political conflict, but its final section, prolonged and dignified, discusses the origins of the Irish dramatic movement. Yeats's participation in this movement was to help him resolve some of the spiritual and political dilemmas presented in earlier sections of *The Trembling of the Veil*, and the divisions of the text reinforce the impression of calm restored after struggle. The text ends on a plateau of structural stability which represents the equilibrium of Yeats's life at this point.

The Trembling of the Veil thus exploits various refined autobiographical techniques, some unique to Yeats and others common to many writers. Yet he finally retreats from any commitment to the self-revelation practised by most autobiographers. The autobiographical protagonist is now highly evasive. His counterpart in *Reveries*, though also fictive, was plausible enough, a passive, talented, often unhappy being who never seriously challenged our usual conception of young Yeats. But in *The Trembling of the Veil* the protagonist is far less tangible. We see him performing aspects of Yeats's life, but we do not feel his responses to experience. After *Reveries* we no longer enjoy the illusion of meeting Yeats's persona on terms of equality—a condition in which we expect to be told everything, though in fact we are not—but are forced to become spectators of a scene much of which we feel to be hidden from us. In *The Trembling of the Veil* everything portends, nothing crystallises. The persona appears correspondingly incapable of fulfilment or independent existence. This attenuated persona serves several purposes: it permits Yeats's dramatisation of London as the realm of other people (his own appropriate habitation being Sligo) and allows him to appear as a detached stage-manager of exemplary lives illustrating the details of his philosophy. Yet at times a reader senses that Yeats has come dangerously close to refining himself out of existence altogether. While *The Trembling of the Veil* remains Yeats's masterpiece in the discursive autobiographical mode, few autobiographical protagonists can have been so elusive. There are several reasons for this reluctance to appear.

First, we should remember Yeats's own caveat about writing of the recent past. Reticence about his relationship to his acquaintances leads him to define them in isolation, as though it were possible to separate his current conception of them from his past knowledge and the historical interaction which had produced it. Such reticence inevitably leaves Yeats's own role in his friends' lives somewhat ill-defined. Moreover, Yeats was indeed discussing a time of fragmented sensibilities: to submit his own character to such a milieu might be dangerous. His apparent reluctance to describe his involvement may, as he claims, reflect an aloofness which he had felt at the time under discussion; as he remarks, 'I see Paris in the Eighteen-nineties as a number of events separated from one another, and without cause or consequence, without lot or part in the logical structure of my life; I can often as little find their dates as I can those of events in my early childhood' (*A* 339).

Second, the authorial persona of a sustained autobiographical text necessarily varies, however slightly, from moment to moment. It is impossible to maintain an absolutely consistent relation to the various phases of one's past. An avowedly 'fictional' account may disguise this problem; in Joyce's *Portrait*, for example, Stephen has sufficient autonomy to make Joyce's fluctuating attitudes to his past self seem a function of Stephen's developing character. In autobiographical texts dealing with distant periods of time (*Reveries*) or with brief experiences, the problem may be avoided. But in *The Trembling of the Veil*, this difficulty is intensified by Yeats's acute awareness of the need to treat different phases of his past in different styles. His ambivalent attitude to his recent past, his knowledge that much material has to be omitted, and his didactic purposes combine to cause reticence and uncertainty in placing and describing himself. His apparent need to write assertively confines him to subjects about which he can assert himself (Yeats's rhetoric always seems designed in part to inhibit or challenge objections); where he doubts his own position he refrains from discussing it, except where he can make doubt itself a subject for emphatic pronouncements.

Finally, it seems that the medium of prose imposes on Yeats assumptions about narrative continuity which make him uncomfortable. He seems especially uneasy when portraying character at length, perhaps because, except in the case of his own character, he prefers to see it as state rather than process. The forms of his memories, 'connected with emotion and place' and therefore 'without sequence' (*A* 5), serve as an excuse to arrange his work impressionistically. Many of the transitions between sections of *The Trembling of the Veil* seem abrupt, as though he would prefer greater freedom to make connections irrespective of narrative logic. The fragmentary endings of several sections of *The Trembling of the Veil*—notably 'Ireland after Parnell' and 'The Tragic Generation', which most conspicuously dramatise the fragmentation of personalities known to Yeats—also contribute to the elusiveness of the central figure. (The effect of these endings is frequently reinforced by imagery suggestive of reversal and decay.) If the Yeats of *The Trembling of the Veil* seems often elusive, he is so partly because Yeats wished he need not present himself with the consistency logically demanded by prose.

Though Yeats persisted with his autobiography, none of the later sections possesses the intensity of *The Trembling of the Veil*. Some were written for specific purposes—to answer his critics or to acknowledge his gratitude for (and worthiness of) the Nobel Prize—and are as much expository or documentary essays as exercises in self-analysis. But Yeats's enthusiasm for working on his declared prose autobiography may also have waned in the later 1920s as he further explored and mastered the art of self-portraiture in his preferred and consummate medium—the lyric poem.

FIVE

Dramatis Personae

WHEN *Dramatis Personae* first appeared in book form it was combined with *Estrangement, The Death of Synge* and *The Bounty of Sweden*, all written some years previously but dealing with periods in Yeats's life which came later than those treated in *Dramatis Personae*; thus his liking for inverted chronology, for reliving his life as it were in reverse, marks this text from the start. One implication of Yeats's title is that the volume will provide a 'dramatis personae' for all the ensuing portions of *Autobiographies*—the three volumes which follow it in the final text—as well as for particular stages of Yeats's life.

Dramatis Personae was not, however, at first combined with Yeats's previously published autobiographical texts, *Reveries over Childhood and Youth* and *The Trembling of the Veil*. But Yeats must already have envisaged, even as he wrote, an eventual fusion with those sections. *Dramatis Personae* completes a process of refutation of George Moore which *Reveries* had begun. In writing *Reveries*, the first section of *Autobiographies* to be composed, Yeats seeks to correct the error Moore had made in claiming that Yeats felt squeamish about his middle-class family background, while in *Dramatis Personae*, the last-written section, he refutes Moore (who was by now safely dead) by presenting the clear implication that Moore's family background was considerably more sullied than his own. *Dramatis Personae*, moreover, is closely linked in structure with *The Trembling of the Veil* just as that text had been structurally linked with its own predecessor, *Reveries*. The two dominant settings treated at the end of *The Trembling of the Veil*, Coole Park and Tulira Castle, are the first places mentioned in *Dramatis Personae*, and Yeats also recapitulates his meetings with Edward Martyn and Lady Gregory, meetings which he had already described in *The Trembling of the Veil*. In this way the two texts are provided with anticipatory structural linkages, of the kind Yeats also used to connect neighbouring poems, even though they were first sent into the world without one another to lean on.

Yeats's plans for *Dramatis Personae* changed radically as the text evolved. In 1926 he was hoping to write a new autobiographical book to treat the years 1900 to 1926; but in 1934, when he finally wrote the book, he covered a much shorter period, essentially 1896–1902. The later part of the period he had planned to cover had now been touched on in his published diary entries, but he probably also found those years difficult to describe in detail. They include the period which was made especially problematic for Yeats by his work in the Abbey Theatre and by Maud Gonne's marriage; Yeats would have seemed less central in an account of this time, even one written by himself, than he had in his depictions of the preceding years. The period he does treat in *Dramatis Personae*, in any case, has its own unity.

Dramatis Personae shows Yeats continuing to implement his plan of depicting his life through accounts of his friends, associates and other contemporaries. The illustrations chosen for the volume emphasise this concern, especially in the earlier versions of the text. These illustrations also enhance the strong 'dramatic' and visual dimension of the volume, Yeats's earnest and graphic process of scene-setting. Further, they complement his highly elaborate descriptions of particular houses, which mostly focus on the paintings they contain. The *London Mercury* version of *Dramatis Personae* contains two portraits of Yeats, one appearing in the first of the three serial instalments and one in the last. This version also contains a portrait of Lady Gregory (by Mrs Jopling) and one of George Moore (by Sir William Rothenstein); both of these appear in the central instalment and so are flanked by the depictions of Yeats himself. The two pictures of Yeats, studied in sequence by the reader, seem to reflect a striking advance in his maturity and dignity; Moore and Lady Gregory, represented by single portraits, seem of course more static. As we have seen, it is typical of autobiographical texts to contrast change in the protagonist with stasis in other people. In the later book version of *Dramatis*

Personae, published by Macmillan in 1936, only the portrait of Lady Gregory remains unaltered. The portrait of Moore is changed to a considerably less flattering one, by W. R. Sickert. (Yeats says of Moore in the text that 'I have in memory Manet's caricature' [*A* 405].) The depictions of Yeats himself are removed, rather as a playwright might forsake the theatre after the first night and allow the drama to operate on its own. Yeats includes, instead, a portrait of Edward Martyn (by Sarah Purser) and his own pastel of Coole House. In the final text of *Autobiographies*, the *Dramatis Personae* section contains only one illustration, the portrait of Lady Gregory, which thus survives, alone and unchanged, in all three versions. Several aspects of these variations in the illustrations to Yeats's texts, however they came about, seem strikingly appropriate to his presentation of himself and others within the prose itself.

This appropriateness is particularly clear where depictions of Yeats are replaced by depictions of his associates (an objective emphasis also present in the text). It is also striking when we reflect on the substitution of a more revealing and much harsher portrait of Moore (the subject of persistent attack in the book), the inclusion in one version of Yeats's own depiction of Coole House (which he describes lovingly, and graphically, in the text as well), and the retention of the same portrait of Lady Gregory, who remains unassailably the book's central figure and whose importance to Yeats stayed crucial and consistent through time. In the final version, Yeats may well have felt that it bestowed more dignity and control on his writing if the tarnished visual images of Moore and Martyn were excised. The removal of their portraits throws additional weight onto Yeats's verbal descriptions of the two men, descriptions which can no longer be countered by the less subjective representations which had been embodied in portraits painted by others. Yeats may have gained confidence that his own descriptions of them would convey the effects he intended, so that the portraits became unnecessary. Moore's independent existence, as a real person rather than as a 'character' depicted satirically by Yeats, thus diminishes perceptibly as the text continues to evolve.

Despite its links with earlier parts of *Autobiographies*, *Dramatis Personae* also embarks in new directions, as seems only appropriate in view of the crucial decade which had passed in Yeats's life since his previous 'new writing' of a part of the autobiography, *The Bounty of Sweden*, which was composed in 1924. (Yeats's writing of *Dramatis Personae* was, in fact, to be his last piece of sustained autobiographical effort in prose.) The focus on other characters apart from Yeats becomes much more consistent and concentrated in *Dramatis Personae* than it had been in the earlier-written parts of *Autobiographies*, and this change is also 'dramatic'. Instead of the diffuse groups of personalities presented discursively and successively in *The Trembling of the Veil*, or the shadowy and sometimes nameless figures who appear in his diary entries, Yeats introduces a trio of more prominent protagonists and directs all his attention at them, setting them energetically in motion and showing them in debate. The text also bears the marks of Yeats's later style—more concrete, immediate and aggressive than his writing in *Reveries over Childhood and Youth* and *The Trembling of the Veil*. This strong style fuses successfully with Yeats's plan to repay George Moore posthumously for his irreverent treatment of Yeats and Lady Gregory, particularly in *Hail and Farewell*. Not only does the style give Yeats's attack considerable intrinsic power and vigour, it also manages by its own nature to disprove much of Moore's testimony, in which Yeats had appeared as shrill, anaemic and flighty, not one who could ever have written the tough and muscular prose of *Dramatis Personae*. The Yeats writing this text, in contrast to the one depicted by Moore, proves himself to be firm and dignified. At the same time, the Moore depicted by Yeats seems largely congruent with the man we envisage when we read Moore's own works. We can be sure that Yeats fully anticipated our responses to all these interrelated perspectives.

Apart from settling accounts with Moore, Yeats also seeks to establish Lady Gregory's own role in his life and in literature. Her house, besides appearing (in Yeats's illustration) in the 1936 edition, is the first location mentioned in the text of *Dramatis Personae*, and is the setting where we tend, with Yeats's encouragement, to envisage most of the scenes in the book taking place. She narrates the 'soliloquy' which Yeats quotes at the end of the final section of the text, and which functions memorably and dramatically to remind us both of her own writing and of her role as a literary patron and helper to Yeats. Grania addressing Diarmuid, in the first passage quoted in this portion of the book, makes us think of Lady Gregory addressing the troubled Yeats who first visited her; in this way the final section of the text recalls, precisely and symmetrically, the opening scenes of *Dramatis Personae*.

Dramatis Personae, as a memoir, thus works to recall lost places as well as lost time. The sense of geography becomes precise and specific, with individually described paintings hanging in particular hallways, something which would not have been depicted in the earlier parts of *Autobiographies*, often marked as they were by Yeats's calculated vagueness of detail. At the beginning of the volume Yeats points out how the great Galway demesnes 'have been divided among small farmers, their great ancient trees cut down' (*A* 385). Yeats's book, like much of his poetry—notably poetry written during that phase of his life which is described in *Dramatis Personae* itself—seeks to reverse this process of disintegration, to recapture Coole as it was: never a striking place architecturally, though of great natural beauty, but a place whose passing we ought all to regret. In *Estrangement*, which follows *Dramatis Personae* in the text of *Autobiographies* but was originally written 25 years earlier, Yeats shows Lady Gregory planting trees at Coole in 1909—perhaps we are led to imagine that these are the same trees whose demise Yeats will report sadly in the 1930s in *Dramatis Personae*. The particular inversion of chronology here (like that involving the first few poems which appear in the *Tower* collection, whose sequence in the volume reverses their order of composition) highlights the sense of times out of joint, of irreparable loss of sacred things, which Yeats presents so energetically in other ways in *Dramatis Personae* and in *Autobiographies* as a whole.

Dramatis Personae thus appears as a complex memoir and polemic which attempts to account for several crucial years in Yeats's life. It also seeks to account for vital years in the development of the Irish theatre, settle a score with an enemy and pay tribute to a friend, and recapture the sense of a setting and a time which have been lost. The successful fusion of these various aims gives the work an intensity and a unity of focus, making it Yeats's most cogent and compelling autobiographical text after *The Trembling of the Veil*. The title *Dramatis Personae*, besides its implications for the structure of *Autobiographies* as a whole, evokes Yeats's involvement in the theatre, and the drama of his life and friendships; and it also acknowledges, quietly, his role as the manipulator of all the figures and scenes he presents.

Since Yeats's text does have such complex and interrelated aims, we can expect to find the kind of structural and textual refinements already encountered in the earlier sections of *Autobiographies*. Many signs of Yeats's attention to such matters are apparent. Yeats's inclusion in the text of letters which he had originally written to Lady Gregory in the 1890s, for example, might seem to guarantee immediacy and precision, by contrast with his manner in *Reveries* (where he claimed he had deliberately avoided the use of letters in order to give his memory free rein). The letters cited in *Dramatis Personae* might seem to be used in order to disprove Moore's view of Yeats with the force of dispassionate, documentary legal evidence. But in fact Yeats revised these letters extensively before citing them in his published text (despite his comment in a letter he wrote to Katharine Tynan in December 1913—just before he began writing declared autobiographical prose—that to 'improve' letters for publication is to act 'in defiance of all right conduct' [*L* 586]). He also begins by quoting certain passages which appear objective and historical, so that we will accept the truth of the quoted matter, then quietly moves onto more controversial ground. In *Dramatis Personae* he accuses Moore of plagiarism, in contrast to his own practice of acknowledging sources; this moral distinction seems slightly qualified by Yeats's canny modes of quoting.

The revisions he makes to these letters never seem massive or deceitful, but they are numerous: in several parts of the text Yeats changes something in every line. Sometimes he shuffles chronology. After citing a letter of 6 November 1898, of course without specifying the date, he says 'then I wrote about "A great battle with George Armstrong"' (*A* 409), which would imply to many readers that he is referring to a passage written the following day or soon afterwards; then he begins citing a letter which had in fact been written months earlier, on 29 June 1898. His general practice here recalls to us, as it probably recalled to him, the revision of his diary entries which he had undertaken in preparing *Estrangement* and *The Death of Synge* a few years earlier. Circumstantial trivia are trimmed, and Yeats and his friends appear with more poise and dignity in the published versions than they had in the original letters. The phrase 'I am in general hot water', for example, is removed from the letter which appears, with numerous other revisions, on *A* 409. Yeats keeps firm control of his presentation here; he quotes extensively from his own letters to others, but not at all from letters he had received. This procedure is of course perfectly proper—he is writing his own autobiography, not those of his friends—but it does give a thoroughly 'Yeatsian' aspect to his correspondence, which may disguise nuances and disagreements which had been present when the letters were originally exchanged. For these reasons the letters can be considered aspects of his present rhetoric as well as documentary fragments from the past. The extracts normally display Yeats's consistent vigour in denouncing philistinism of various kinds. One set of revised letters appears in the text immediately after his account of the financial support he had received from Lady Gregory, and is presumably cited in order to illustrate how worthy he had been of such support. The letters also stress his gratitude to Lady Gregory and his awareness of her real sympathy (even though, as Yeats remarks, 'those who did not know her thought her stern' [*A* 412]; thus Yeats's ability to perceive her true nature is meant to show his wisdom, as well as reminding us of the closeness of his friendship with her).

As he had done in earlier parts of *Autobiographies*, Yeats presents a few scenes in particularly short sections of text for emphasis, as with his first mention of the theatrical activity which becomes a central subject of *Dramatis Personae* (*A* 388), the introduction of Florence Farr and of Yeats's attempt 'to revive the ancient art of minstrelsy' (*A* 407), and his account of the opening night of *The Bending of the Bough* (*A* 429–30). Some affinity between his division of text into sections and the use of short dramatic scenes in a play must also have been in Yeats's mind from the outset: he begins his fifth section of text by saying, 'When I went to Coole the curtain had fallen upon the first act of my drama' (*A* 395). Several sections of *Dramatis*

Personae begin with scene-setting, conspicuously the first: Yeats dramatically ends his opening paragraph 'Then I saw the great trees, then the grey wall of the Castle' (*A* 385). The third section opens with a shift to Lady Gregory's house: 'A glimpse of a long vista of trees, over an undergrowth of clipped laurels, seen for a moment as the outside car approached her house on my first visit, is a vivid memory' (*A* 388). Yeats's account of a public dinner becomes drama (or farce) in the juxtaposition of John F. Taylor and George Moore: Taylor's 'body was angular, often rigid with suppressed rage, his gaze fixed upon some object, his clothes badly made, his erect attitude suggesting a firm base. Moore's body was insinuating, upflowing, circulative, curvicular, pop-eyed' (*A* 422). This cacophony of subtly dismissive adjectives, contrasting strikingly with Yeats's usual sinewy style in *Dramatis Personae* (and perhaps, ingeniously, operating as a parodically heightened version of Yeats's manner of writing as Moore had exaggerated and distorted it in his own account) actually comes to characterise Moore. Yeats reinforces this impression by adding a few pages later the judgment that 'as convert [Moore] was embarrassing, unsubduable, preposterous' (*A* 427).

Yeats carefully heightens the contrast between Lady Gregory and Moore (sometimes he teams Martyn with Moore, partly to enhance Lady Gregory's contrasting dignity and partly to give himself a larger and jollier target). Moore's vulgarity, randomness, lack of individuality ('more mob than man' [*A* 431]) and pallid shapelessness ('carved out of a turnip' [*A* 405]) contrast with Lady Gregory's dignity and integrity (also, implicitly, with Yeats's own). Moore remains content with chaos, equivocation, compromise and absurdity—as Yeats shows in his ludicrous anecdote about the cycling Moore's recurrently falling underwear [*A* 405])—while Lady Gregory calmly insists that 'the only wrong act that matters is not doing one's best work' (*A* 408), a sentiment which Yeats would certainly endorse and seek to exemplify. Yeats's citation of such trivial anecdotes involving Moore also seems a parody of Moore's avowed theory and practice of literary naturalism.

Moore lacks taste, despite his large estate and his professed interest in painting (it may be in part to satirise Moore's general lack of taste that in *Dramatis Personae* Yeats dwells, lingeringly, uncharacteristically and rather unconvincingly, on his own sensitive responses to various paintings). Martyn, for all that he lives at Tulira Castle, 'hated that house in all its detail' (*A* 386). Lady Gregory, by contrast, quietly appreciates the value of her house and of the painstakingly collected objects it contains; and Yeats shows his own appreciation of the dignity of the great houses. Since *Dramatis Personae* has such a specific, restricted and thoroughly delineated geographical setting, these attitudes to houses come to seem reliable guides to character. They also accord with Yeats's evaluations elsewhere in his writing, as in his poem 'In Memory of Eva Gore-Booth and Con Markiewicz', for example. While Martyn appears in Yeats's account simultaneously degenerate and ascetic by comparison with his more spirited ancestors and especially his amorous father, Lady Gregory seems the fitting inheritor of her family's past and the past of her husband's family. (Incidentally, Yeats's juxtaposition of Moore, Martyn and Lady Gregory also makes a convincing case, even to readers who might be doubtful initially, that this kind of aristocratic attentiveness to places and traditions has intrinsic merit; Lady Gregory's awareness in this area correlates with her general sensitivity, while Moore's and Martyn's obtuseness accords with their lack of taste in most other matters.) Yeats wishes particularly to correct Moore's highly condescending portrayal of Lady Gregory in *Hail and Farewell*, and he does so at the same time by convincingly presenting her in a more positive way than Moore's and by demonstrating Moore's complete incompetence as a witness. It is a deadly and successful method; Yeats opposes his own depictions of Lady Gregory and of Moore himself precisely to Moore's own characterisations. He thus puts Moore to use in a way Moore would have found exasperating.

Yeats contrives to place himself on the side of the angels. Moore had claimed that Yeats's mind and heart had diverged, but in *Dramatis Personae* Yeats depicts himself convincingly as a whole and calm person, by contrast with the chaotic, centrifugal, breathless Moore. Yeats shows his own affinities with Coole Park, whose beauty he fully appreciates, as his poetry also demonstrates. Lady Gregory comes to embody Yeats's graciousness as well as her own, in a method of self-depiction which Yeats had already employed in *The Trembling of the Veil*. Yeats had earlier defended himself from Moore's attacks on his social attitudes in writing *Reveries* and his poetry collection *Responsibilities*, but now he also shows himself to be a truer aristocrat than Moore or Martyn. Of Martyn, Yeats reflects that 'two traditions met and destroyed each other in his blood, creating the sterility of a mule' (*A* 388). His treatment of Moore's lineage can be equally harsh:

> Moore's grandfather or great-grandfather had been a convert, but there were Catholic marriages. Catholic families, beaten down by the Penal Laws, despised by Irish Protestants, by the few English Catholics they met, had but little choice as to where they picked their brides; boys, on one side of old family, grew up squireens, half-sirs, peasants who had lost their tradition, gentlemen who had lost theirs. Lady Gregory once told me what marriage coarsened the Moore blood, but I have forgotten. (*A* 402)

This seems a typically calculated piece of supposed forgetfulness on Yeats's part, of course; he would have recalled the detail effortlessly if it had not been considerably more appropriate and striking to omit it. Here Yeats risks descending to Moore's rhetorical level as he himself had depicted it. In his 1913 diary Yeats had noted that Moore's father 'was a man of education and power and old descent', a point favourable to Moore which Yeats studiously omits from his published text.[1] Yeats does include a few tepid and backhanded tributes to Moore, thus slightly softening the attack: 'Moore in his moments of self-abnegation was convinced and convincing' (*A* 426). (From Yeats's account, of course, we would suspect such moments to have been infrequent with Moore; we might also reflect that self-abnegation is a quality which Yeats never particularly admired.) Yeats may also wish to show here that he can be more magnanimous than Martyn, who had apparently denied that Moore possessed any good points at all (*A* 401). Yeats even manages to compare himself favourably with Moore by adopting a self-deprecatory tone: 'I had read no book of [Moore's], nor would I, had he not insisted, for my sympathies were narrow. I cared for nothing but poetry or prose that shared its intensity' (*A* 407). This confessed 'narrowness' of taste must, however, be preferred to Moore's vague, random enthusiasms, and Yeats also manages to label Moore's prose (even while confessing that he has never read it) as deficient in intensity.

Yeats's observation that Moore 'sacrificed all that seemed to other men good breeding, honour, friendship, in pursuit of what he considered the root facts of life' (*A* 403) recalls that in *Dramatis Personae* Yeats's own breeding, honour, and capacity for friendship receive strong and convincing emphasis, as indeed they do throughout *Autobiographies*. At the beginning of *Dramatis Personae* Yeats links the development of his own life from one phase to another with the state of the great houses at corresponding times: 'When I was thirty years old the three great demesnes of three Galway houses, Coole House, Tulira Castle, Roxborough House, lay within a half-hour or two hours' walk of each other' (*A* 385). Here, Yeats implies his familiarity (and affinity) with the great houses; it is as if when he was thirty years old he had already acquired the habit of walking among them. The triple repetition of variants of 'three', in the references to three demesnes, three houses, and Yeats's own thirty years, reinforces the impression that Yeats had become closely associated with aristocratic places when he was still a young man. Strikingly, the phrase 'thirty years' appears not only in the first line of *Dramatis Personae* but also in the first line of *The Bounty of Sweden*, which of course was written earlier; most readers will no doubt miss the echo, but if noticed it must reinforce our sense of Yeats's dignity and of the continuity between early promise and later achievement. A similar contrast between Yeats and Moore is also hinted in *The Death of Synge*, where Yeats remarks 'I once said to George Moore, "Synge has always the better of you, for you have brief but ghastly moments during which you admit the existence of other writers; Synge never has"' (*A* 512). This passage deftly contrasts Moore's motley, insecure personality with Yeats's own calm demeanour, esteem for Synge, and sense of humour. In this case, too, Moore is given no right of reply within Yeats's text (published at a time when Moore was still alive); whereas in *Dramatis Personae* (published after his death) Moore condemns himself in every speech Yeats attributes to him.

By contrast with Moore's blundering promiscuity, Yeats

emphasises his own staunch, elegant devotion to a romantic ideal: 'I disliked Moore's now sentimental, now promiscuous amours, the main matter of his talk. A romantic, when romanticism was in its final extravagance, I thought one woman, whether wife, mistress, or incitement to platonic love, enough for a lifetime' (*A* 431). Earlier, more specifically, he had explained his largely unreciprocated passion for Maud Gonne in terms of his relationship with the spirit of the age: 'My devotion might as well have been offered to an image in a milliner's window, or to a statue in a museum, but romantic doctrine had reached its extreme development' (*A* 399). Even in the romantic or sexual sphere, then, where Yeats might appear to some observers less enterprising or successful than Moore, he seeks to demonstrate not only his superior nobility and dignity—further illustrated by his escape from Dowson's fate of dissipation after a rejection which should logically have been less traumatic than Yeats's rejection by Maud Gonne—but his sensitivity to the demands made by the mood of the time.

The mood of the time could not, of course, always suffice as a guide to conduct, either direct or ironic. Occasionally, in the public sphere, it must be simply opposed, and Yeats values his own play *The Countess Cathleen* for its willingness to challenge the accepted tastes of the day: ' *The Heather Field* was a much greater success than *The Countess Cathleen*, being in the manner of Ibsen, the manner of the moment' (*A* 417). (Yeats also found Bernard Shaw too well-suited to the spirit of the age for his own good.) But it is *The Countess Cathleen*, not *The Heather Field*, which will endure, for in challenging the age it establishes a firm beachhead for itself, while the popular *Heather Field* will simply drift with the current of fashion. Yeats implicitly contrasts his own highly-wrought and therefore permanent texts with Moore's amorphous writing; Moore's work, like Davidson's, is unmemorable, for Moore's 'nature, bitter, violent, discordant, did not fit him to write the sentences men murmur again and again for years' (*A* 438). Yeats's own sentence describing Moore's failure to become memorable manages, itself, to be highly memorable, becoming by such means the more persuasive. Yeats's final anti-Moore strategy rests, with a serenity which might have infuriated Moore had he lived to see it, upon the rhetorical ease and control manifest in his whole text, apart from the specific refutations of Moore included in it. *Dramatis Personae* itself shows not only Yeats's superiority to Moore, but also, more satisfyingly, Yeats's skill in putting Moore to use: as an antagonist against whom Yeats can continue to define himself dramatically, yet personally.

SIX

Estrangement and *The Death of Synge*

A READER turning to *Estrangement* and *The Death of Synge* after looking at *Dramatis Personae* may be uncertain how to respond. Both of these new sections begin with gnomic, cryptic utterances. *The Death of Synge*, in particular, opens with a rhetorical question, a device which Yeats uses more typically at the close of a text than at the beginning. There is thus an odd sense of marmoreal finality at the outset, which faintly echoes the inverted chronology operating at the opening of *Dramatis Personae*; though Yeats's rhetorical question in *The Death of Synge* now hints at a movement away from the tensions expressed in the preceding sections (*Dramatis Personae* and *Estrangement*) and towards greater compassion: 'Why does the struggle to come at truth take away our pity, and the struggle to overcome our passions restore it again?' (*A* 499).

We might nevertheless detect in these sections a falling-off in tension, a sense of Yeats's declining interest in the autobiography and an increasing reluctance to make extensive creative efforts (though we should also, of course, remember that these sections were actually prepared for publication some years before *Dramatis Personae* was written). The reader may even feel estranged from the writing.

It could also be argued, however, that such changes in emphasis are entirely appropriate, that they reflect precisely the shape of Yeats's life at the period he is discussing in these texts and perhaps, also, at the period when they were revised for publication. It would be fascinating to discover to what extent Yeats consciously believed in the efficacy of such mimetic methods of conveying the outlines of his life; to discover whether he envisaged, or wanted, that sense of estrangement or alienation which many readers do feel as they confront these

strange and craggy texts. It is an appropriate correlative to this
method that Yeats should always have refrained from directly
discussing such possibilities; yet they may well have occurred
to him. The opening passage of *Estrangement* talks about the
limitations of books as a mode of self-portraiture, and hints at
the advantages which may accrue from more flexible forms of
communication. Thus we might feel encouraged to see the
present text as a self-conscious exploration of such forms. At the
same time, Yeats seems characteristically disingenuous here,
since he begins his text by explicitly decrying modes of rhetoric
which he then blithely proceeds to employ.

Although these sections seem so uncompromising and
autonomous, they do resemble other parts of *Autobiographies* in
certain respects, as Yeats's subtle introduction obliquely hints.
If we take the section called *Dramatis Personae* with them, as the
book version issued in 1936 with the collective title *Dramatis
Personae* in fact did, we can say that the three parts form a
triptych anticipating the configuration of portraits which Yeats
presents explicitly in *The Bounty of Sweden* ('I felt that a young
man's ghost should have stood upon one side of me and at the
other a living woman sinking into the infirmity of age' [*A* 571]).
Dramatis Personae appears as a depiction of Lady Gregory and
The Death of Synge, obviously, as a depiction of Synge; between
these two sections *Estrangement* mostly shows Yeats's own
estrangement, and so we can envisage him standing in the book
(as well as in his Stockholm lecture, in the theatre, and in life
generally) between the two admired figures to whom he pays
clear tribute later. This triptych also makes an appearance, in
exactly the same configuration, in the poetry, where Yeats
refers to 'John Synge, I and Augusta Gregory' (*CP* 369), his
own centrality reinforced by the unusual word order.

In *Estrangement* and *The Death of Synge* there is a movement
outwards from the private to the public realm, a movement
which also occurs in other parts of *Autobiographies*—perhaps
especially *The Trembling of the Veil*—and through the book as a
whole. And although *Estrangement* and *The Death of Synge* seem
the most fragmentary sections of *Autobiographies*, the ones which
communicate in the most impressionistic and least logical
manner, we might reflect that an emphasis on impressionism
rather than logic has marked the text from the beginning;

Autobiographies begins with Yeats's reflection 'My first memories are fragmentary and isolated and contemporaneous, as though one remembered some first moments of the Seven Days' (*A* 5), and literary modes which seem congruent with the manner of these 'first memories' appear from time to time throughout the book.

The texts collected in *Estrangement* and *The Death of Synge* purport to be diary entries—usually a 'private' form of writing, which we may feel mildly voyeuristic in broaching—and the authenticity of the claim can be established: the passages, or passages very like them, were indeed part of Yeats's diary at one time. Yet they are presented for us now as a finished text, and as part of a longer work (*Autobiographies*) even though, rather disconcertingly, no commentary explicitly links them to that longer work. They do have their own kind of coherence, and they may even seem to some readers to form a more smoothly finished unity than *Dramatis Personae*, which occasionally sounds splenetic or erratic in tone. The fact that Yeats suppresses explicit associations, so that the reader must make the effort to connect the sections of text together and to their context in *Autobiographies*, also seems appropriate.

Yeats was busy with many projects in the late 1920s. As we have seen, it is obvious from a study of *Dramatis Personae* that he continued to find it difficult to write explicit accounts of his life in the early part of the century. Thus, when he felt he should add a section to his autobiography which would cover the years 1909–14, it was logical for him to turn to the diary he had kept at that time to provide material. Despite the implicit claim of immediacy and historical authenticity conveyed by this method, however, Yeats worked over his text to make it accord with the rest of *Autobiographies* and to hone his rhetorical purposes, just as he was to do with the letters he quotes—with revisions—in *Dramatis Personae*. *Estrangement* and *The Death of Synge* are among the most extensively reworked sections of the whole book; though this fact may seem inevitable given Yeats's reticence and the nature of the text's origins in an actual diary not at first intended for publication. Still, there remain some repetitions of material treated earlier in *Autobiographies*, which may occasionally show inattentive revision rather than rhetorical purpose. For example, Yeats repeats (*A* 468) an anecdote about his fellow-student at art school who wore a daisy-chain around his neck, an anecdote which he had already given in *Reveries* (*A* 80); and while the story may be apt enough at each occurrence, it is difficult to see any reasons for the repetition as such.

Yeats seems to have worked energetically at transforming a private manner into a public one. Yet even in its earliest form his diary may well have been intended for another reader's attention as well as his own: a letter to Florence Farr implies that she was meant to see it, and he probably wanted Maud Gonne as another witness. The diary would therefore serve, like his letters, to demonstrate to Maud Gonne his earnestness, dedication and insight. It is, nevertheless, possible that Yeats's references to other readers applied only to particular passages and not to the diary as a whole.

Yeats also intended his diary as a seedbed or nursery for material destined to be published later: draft poems and notes for essays and lectures appear in it from time to time. Thus it never was a wholly private affair. Rather it was concerned, both structurally and thematically, with the relationship of public and private worlds. Yeats seems to have made surprisingly little distinction between these areas in his manner of address: despite his own remarks contrasting private poetry and public rhetoric, he apparently retained his characteristically declamatory manner even when writing for himself alone. The manner always seems a necessity of his personality rather than a function of his sense of audience, and thus it might well survive even in places where no external audience was anticipated. Perhaps *First Draft* best illustrates this contention, though parts of even that supposedly private text were certainly written with eventual translation to the public domain prominently in mind. We might compare an attribute of Yeats's character Michael which is mentioned in the 'De Burgh' version of *The Speckled Bird*: 'Years of solitude had made him talkative instead of silent, and part of his power of moving others came from his talking to them as if he were talking to himself' (*SB* 209). Yeats makes a similar remark in his own person in a letter to Katharine Tynan: 'I like to write to you as if talking to myself' (*L* 83).

Yeats never intended his diary to be merely a day-by-day record of events. He aims to avoid sequence and the demands of 'logical process', recording only moments of significance. Daily events actually appear more often in his letters, which may have been designed in part to siphon off such ephemera so that the diary remained an unencumbered vessel suited to more substantial concerns. Even in the diary, Yeats reveals his persistent inclination to order his experience, to give it formal coherence through his manner of recording it. Though an engaging frankness, exceeding anything found in the letters, often asserts itself, a frankness destined only for his own eyes or those of a relatively sympathetic female witness like Florence Farr or even Maud Gonne falls short of public confession. 'It is always inexcusable to lose one's self-possession', he notes (*M* 138), a remark which by its rather claustrophobic primness manages to suggest that in some circumstances it might be much better if one did lose one's self-possession. He observes that 'I fear strangers; I fear the representatives of the collective opinion, and so rage stupidly and rudely, exaggerating what I feel and think' (*M* 138); his regret here sounds authentic enough. He complains of an inability to concentrate, of nerves, of his compulsive need to convince: 'I want to convince instead of being satisfied to be obeyed' (*M* 167); in other words, power over others only pleases him when it is intellectual as well as practical. He accuses himself of failure to trust, boastfulness, indiscretion, inattentiveness, indolence, indecision, bad temper and arrogance. He stresses the therapeutic value which such self-critical observations may have: 'I dare say that these notes, if some chance eye light on them, may seem morbid; but they help me to understand myself, and I remember hearing a man of science once argue that all progress is at the outset "pathological". I know that I have already made moral gains' (*M* 190). The throwaway remark 'if some chance eye light on them' implies that he does expect such an eye to appear at a later stage, and also adds emphasis to his definition of the diary as an aid to self-understanding. The devices he uses in letters to disguise weaknesses from others and from himself seldom appear, though one sometimes senses a slightly wistful exaggeration of the deficiency, as if to prompt—if only from himself or his sympathetic female audience of one—a silent reassurance that he may in fact be less reprehensible than he claims.

Amusingly, Yeats hints in his diary at an intermittent irritability about letter-writing, a mood which he usually manages to keep out of the letters themselves; his entry for 28 February 1909 reads 'Letters. Tired out. 11:15 to 1:15, Letters. 2:30 to 3:30, Letters' (*M* 174). Sometimes he admits into his text an appealing intimacy: 'I must stop writing and lie down, or go out and walk. I have the old stopping of my faculties when I ask for serious thought' (*M* 160). He reflects on the theatre and indulges in astrological speculations. Dutifully, he records his dreams, and other people's dreams, sometimes checking with the dreamer later to ensure that he has recorded the details correctly. He notes his evaluations of and reactions to other people's behaviour as it impinges, often irritatingly, on his own aspirations; thus emphasis will often be thrown on how he is prevented from acting rather than on how he acts, and another observer describing Yeats at the same period would undoubtedly have depicted him as considerably more self-willed and productive than he appears in his own account. This emphasis on the effect of others on him, rather than of himself on others, illustrates the common pattern in which autobiographical protagonists appear passive—partly because they usually spend so much of their time recording what has happened to them.

The extensive changes which Yeats made to his diary entries when preparing *Estrangement* and *The Death of Synge* for publication reveal much about his notion of truth and his attitudes to his audience. Occasionally he makes the text sound more immediate and personal, closer to the manner we might have expected to find in a diary, than the original diary had been. For instance, the sententious 'I must keep one note from leading on to another. To do that is to surrender oneself to literature' (*M* 139) becomes the slightly more modest, reflective and personal 'I must keep one note from leading on to another, that I may not surrender myself to literature' (*A* 461); this change is trivial enough, but it is fascinating to see the direction in which it moves, and similar examples abound. He deletes some formal sentences from the diary: 'Mere wisdom would die, he knows, like any other living breath' (*M* 147). He adds a few hints of colloquialism or tentativeness which the original text had lacked—the phrase 'I think', for example (*A* 476, *M* 159). On the other hand, Yeats does excise in revision many personal references, some of the passages of self-criticism, and the diverse, ephemeral matter which in the diary had cast light on the details of his life. The revealing sentence 'All my worst faults of self-assertion and temper come from being too indolent and careless to keep a distance between myself and men and women in all those things where they are my inferiors' (*M* 155) disappears in the *Autobiographies* text, as does the reflection 'I begin to wonder whether I have and always have had some nervous weakness inherited from my mother' (*M* 156). The published version thus presents a more amicable, poised, consistent, detached personality. Yeats only retains allusions to those faults in himself which he can gain some credit from specifying.

Yeats removes most personal names from his account in revision, replacing them with randomly selected initials. It may seem strange that he should expect readers to take an interest in his personal descriptions even when they are unsure of the identity of his subjects, but this revision does make the work more cogent in a sense by throwing emphasis onto Yeats's manner of judgment rather than the details of the actual personalities being judged. The revision thus moves Yeats's account further into the subjective realm, much as his habit of quoting from his own letters—but nobody else's—does in *Dramatis Personae*. It also deprives contemporary readers of the opportunity to dispute his evaluations; though such a response was probably not to be expected in any case, since sixteen years had elapsed between the writing of the diary and its appearance in print.

Estrangement and *The Death of Synge* thus present a public, exemplary Yeats distilled from the more random self of the 1909–14 diary. Refined, concentrated prose style reflects his evolution between 1909 and the late 1920s, and so recalls his manner to the present; the style itself, that is, operates in an autobiographical manner, suggesting that the changes in Yeats which he shows as occurring in 1909–14 had in fact continued until the time of writing. He suppresses self-criticism partly out of reticence but also, one suspects, because he no longer felt it to apply. Certainly he had changed greatly in the intervening period, which included the time of his marriage, and some of the harshness and brittleness which Yeats (and various other witnesses) felt he displayed early in the century had no doubt softened over the years.

In the diary he had incorporated criticism of others as well as of himself; even the greatly admired Synge appears sometimes in an unflattering light (as at *M* 201–2). The removal of such passages, now made necessary by tact and decorum, also justified and required the excision of self-criticism, so that he should not seem unduly, even masochistically, harsh in evaluating his own past behaviour. Meditations on his character mostly become more general in the course of revision. Yet he adds remarkably little material to the diary, as if he wants the past merely refined, not reconstructed. He can hardly have had philosophical scruples about adding material, since some of the changes and deletions he makes alter the facts—and incorporate new emphases—quite as strikingly as minor additions could have done. In *The Death of Synge* he deftly arranges around a thematic focus material which had seemed much more heterogeneous in the original version.

Yeats includes in *Estrangement* an account of his belief 'that vice does not destroy genius but that the heterogeneous does' (*A* 484). This statement expresses one of Yeats's central themes in all his work, that the writer of genius must struggle against disorder; and *Estrangement* itself, by demonstrating Yeats's ability to make a cogent text out of a more miscellaneous one, embodies the belief convincingly.

Ronsley has remarked that 'in the individual experience the face one presents to the world often plays a greater part than either the more instinctive self behind it or the external world's expectations of behavior'.[1] A similar realisation colours Yeats's self-presentation both in the diary and in its published descendants. The faults of which he accuses himself mostly involve the way he has appeared to the world in a specific situation, as though it required a public rebuff or awkwardness to make him realise that his behaviour had been questionable. Thus the face he presents to the world becomes the testing-ground for his assumptions about conduct; and the diary is essentially a means of meditating on the interplay between public and private worlds, symbolised by the conflict between the face one would like to assume and the expressions which are forced on it by contact with society. Yeats thus brings to a precise focus, within these apparently abrupt and gritty texts, some of the central thematic preoccupations of *Autobiographies*.

SEVEN

The Bounty of Sweden

THE FINAL section of *Autobiographies* has seemed to some readers to be a coda or an afterthought, scarcely integrated with the other parts of the text; some have even suspected that Yeats placed *The Bounty of Sweden* here simply because he needed a home for it. It is cooler and more detached in tone than some earlier sections, though this difference could be attributed to Yeats's greater poise and self-assurance at the moment of writing (just after he had received the Nobel Prize), or to his desire to appear in full possession of such qualities. The coolness and detachment, some readers might say, also accord with and reflect the Swedish setting.

In fact, however, *The Bounty of Sweden* was designed at the outset as a part of Yeats's autobiography. When Yeats notes in its second paragraph that he plans to write out his Swedish recollections 'as in a kind of diary' (*A* 531), he may already have anticipated the linking of this section with his revised diary entries which were to appear in *Estrangement* and *The Death of Synge*, prepared for publication a few years later, and eventually placed in *Autobiographies* immediately before the Swedish section. In all these sections, the impression that we are reading diary entries leads us to assume a spontaneity of response which can be revealed, bibliographically, as a deliberate Yeatsian construction achieved largely by his judicious revision of his original texts. The phrase 'thirty years' with which the first part of the Swedish section begins is echoed at the opening of the sixth part, and this parallel seems, when we read *Autobiographies* in sequence, to reinforce the echo of the beginning of *Dramatis Personae*, where (as we have already seen) the phrase appears once more. Yeats's inclusion of his Nobel lecture on the Irish dramatic movement as part of *The Bounty of*

Sweden also links his Swedish section tightly to *Dramatis Perso-nae*, which discusses the same movement. This link must have seemed especially striking in the original version of the book published under the title *Dramatis Personae*, which begins with the section we now know by that name and ends with the lecture, so reinforcing in its structure the pattern in which Yeats's own assessments subsume objective realities.

Moreover, in the first paragraph of *The Bounty of Sweden* Yeats refers to MacGregor Mathers and Synge, figures who appear prominently in other sections of *Autobiographies*, thus linking those sections with this new writing. Yeats's phrase and image 'that final consummate strength which rounds the spiral of a shell' (*A* 540) recalls precisely that passage, already quoted, in *The Trembling of the Veil*: 'Is it not certain that the Creator yawns in earthquake and thunder and other popular displays, but toils in rounding the delicate spiral of a shell?' (*A* 249). It is also possible to argue that *The Bounty of Sweden* echoes the section 'The Stirring of the Bones' in particular; both texts treat similar concerns, and both end with accounts of the Irish dramatic movement. Both titles, perhaps coincidentally, emphasise the initial letters 'B' and 'S', as the title *The Speckled Bird* had also done; and Yeats discusses *The Speckled Bird*, which he seldom mentions elsewhere in his published work, within 'The Stirring of the Bones' itself (*A* 376). We might see 'The Stirring of the Bones' as a preliminary summation of Yeats's chief concerns in *Autobiographies*, an impression further enhanced by the way its title echoes in structure the title of the volume containing it, *The Trembling of the Veil*. *The Bounty of Sweden*, then, appears as a more definitive summary of Yeats's preoccupations. *The Bounty of Sweden* also fits itself into the patterns of the whole volume, *Autobiographies*, by reverting to the use of the present tense, which Yeats had employed at the opening of *Reveries over Childhood and Youth*.

Besides, *The Bounty of Sweden* develops and brings to a precise and satisfying conclusion many broader elements of the whole book. Yeats's thematic preoccupation with the contrast bet-ween youth and age links the volume with the rest of the autobiography and especially with *The Trembling of the Veil*; as he examines his Nobel Prize medal, for example, he reflects of its pictured youth that 'I was good-looking once like that young man, but my unpractised verse was full of infirmity, my Muse old as it were; and now I am old and rheumatic, and nothing to look at, but my Muse is young. I am even persuaded that she is like those Angels in Swedenborg's vision, and moves perpetually "towards the day-spring of her youth"' (*A* 541).

The Nobel Prize itself appears as a fitting capstone to Yeats's career; and his account of the presentation ceremony appears as a fitting capstone to his account of that career. The procedure adopted at the Nobel prizegiving, in which Yeats has to make an awkward progress up a flight of steps and keep a wary eye over his shoulder, now becomes in his account of it a neat retrospective symbol for his stance and mode of progress in his autobiographical writing from the beginning: difficult, steady, upward, purposive and circumspect. His comments on Swedish architecture often suggest an analogy with his construction of *Autobiographies* itself, in which process various minute and apparently discrete particulars had gradually but steadily fused into an aesthetic whole: 'Among all these irrelevant associations . . . I discover at last a vast, dominating, unconfused outline, a masterful simplicity' (*A* 542–3).

Yeats's title for the section leads us inevitably to contrast the bounty or generosity of Sweden, as presented here at the conclusion of his text, with the meanness of Ireland as it appears in several of the other sections of *Autobiographies*. Sweden's generosity, of course, involves more than the Nobel Prize, fit emblem though that seems; it also appears in popular Swedish attitudes to the individual prize winners and to literature, art, culture and education. That this contrast was deliberate, and was vital to Yeats, can be confirmed by the fact that the sections of *Autobiographies* most emphatically depicting Irish meanness are those compiled or written later than the Swedish section—*Dramatis Personae*, *Estrangement* and *The Death of Synge* (whose increasingly bleak titles prepare in the text for the striking effusion of *The Bounty of Sweden*, both the title and the book). Shirley Neuman suggests: 'That it is appropriate for Yeats to adopt the mask of Castiglione in this court where it seemed but affectation in modern Ireland makes for much of the difference between the stridency of *Estrangement* and the graciousness of *The Bounty of Sweden*'.[1] And, as Ronsley remarks in his account of *The Bounty of Sweden*, Yeats's 'first conversation after leaving England centers on Danish education that makes "examinations almost nothing and the personality of the teacher almost everything" and that rouses "the imagination with Danish literature and history"'.[2] Yeats's description here of an admirable mode of education practised in Scandinavia contrasts with his depiction, near the beginning of *Autobiographies*, of the more limiting education he himself had received in Ireland (and in England). It also contrasts with a strong attack on the limitations of Irish education (which he claims 'substitutes pedantry for taste' [*A* 500]) included in *The Death of Synge* and consequently destined to appear, in the final version of *Autobiographies*, just thirty pages before the opening of *The Bounty of Sweden*. He begins *The Bounty of Sweden* by referring to Paris—a place which he seldom discusses elsewhere in his writings—perhaps in order to preface his remarks about Stockholm by alluding to another city which is more universally regarded as a centre of light and culture (though he had mentioned Paris less positively in *The Trembling of the Veil* [*A* 339]). He implicitly contrasts the style of Paris with the style (or lack of style) found in Dublin and London, again anticipating the contrast which becomes the basis for *The Bounty of Sweden* (and recalling the manner of contrasting places which he had used in *John Sherman*).

Yeats presents Sweden as a place of culture, and more emphatically, as a place where culture has a positive effect on a whole population. No doubt his actual response to Stockholm during his visit in 1923 included a genuine appreciation of such qualities, and other witnesses have made similar observations. Yet it is also striking that Yeats's account of the city fits neatly into the existing, evolving pattern formed by his depictions of ideal, artistic city-states, such as Urbino and Byzantium, places which have attained unity of being and unity of culture, and which can be contrasted with Dublin. He mentions Byzantium specifically within the text of *The Bounty of Sweden* itself: in the Stockholm Town Hall, he observes, 'there is no important French influence, for all that has not come out of the necessities of site and material, no matter in what school the artist studied, carries the mind backward to Byzantium' (*A* 554). Byzantium also appears prominently in poems which Yeats wrote soon after his return from Stockholm, and his presentation of his partly imaginary Byzantium may well be coloured by his actual experience of the Swedish city.

One detail reflecting Yeats's ability—conscious in a given case or not—to organise textual elements with great subtlety appears towards the end of the volume. Stockholm impresses him with its beauty, but local people lament that he has not seen it at its best, elegantly covered with snow. Instead, there is central heating everywhere, a trivial fact recalling the house-drains mentioned earlier in *Autobiographies*, not conducive to cold passion, and likely to melt the snow so that it appears only as slush—real life constantly peeping amorphously through. This passage strikingly recalls his mention, near the beginning of *Autobiographies*, of the painting his father had once spoiled by incorporating seasonal variations until, at his winter sittings, the snow he felt obliged to add promptly obliterated all the details of the earlier seasons. Then, chill perfection was somehow lifeless, while real life changed and burgeoned, if only the artist could manage to convey it. Now, that kind of frosty perfection is sought, at least by the citizens of Stockholm. But Yeats has quietly reoriented himself in the meantime. It had taken him many years to accommodate himself to the contingency and shapelessness of life, but in *The Bounty of Sweden*, as in the 'Crazy Jane' poems and in *Last Poems* generally, he shows his conviction that these qualities are his reality, are the place where all the ladders start. It now seems altogether appropriate to celebrate the news of the Nobel Prize by cooking sausages rather than uncorking wine (*A* 533). The admirable qualities of Stockholm must be slightly qualified by this recognition, which also colours Yeats's depictions of Byzantium in the ensuing years—especially in the poem 'Byzantium' (*CP* 280), where the city has become vital and even violent.

The involution which marks much of *Autobiographies* reaches an apt culmination in *The Bounty of Sweden*. The ending of Yeats's lecture on the Irish dramatic movement pays tribute to Synge and Lady Gregory, and places Yeats himself firmly between them and at the centre of the movement; these emphases focus precisely the concerns of *The Bounty of Sweden* as a whole, and, more generally, those of the entire volume. And if *Autobiographies* had begun in a Joycean manner, it ends similarly: Yeats's use of his own lecture shows him fusing with his text, as Stephen Dedalus does in the diary entries which appear at the end of the *Portrait*.

Yeats's increasing objectivity appears in the narrative tone and angle of *The Bounty of Sweden*. The reader is encouraged to read the text in much the same spirit Yeats had experienced as he approached Stockholm: curiously and reverently and with few preconceptions, perhaps not recognising the application of the descriptions to immediate contexts until it is made fully explicit—rather as Yeats failed to recognise, until someone drew the fact to his attention, that a crowd had gathered for the purpose of looking at him.

Yeats does not comment on how we should react to anything he tells us; his manner is wittily distanced throughout the section, as if he refrains from attempts to control our responses, and the volume ends on a comic note reflecting Yeats's current mature serenity of perception (a mimetic autobiographical manner) as well as the process of conquering anxiety, a process which *Autobiographies* as a whole has traced. The comic, brisk and cheerful manner also shows Yeats drawing back from immediate physical concerns to meditate on the course of his life: a most appropriate tone to adopt at the conclusion of his central piece of sustained self-scrutiny, *Autobiographies*.

EIGHT

Behind the Lines

SINCE autobiographical writing always involves a great deal of self-consciousness, it readily becomes highly self-aware and self-observing.[1] Authorial assumptions about self-portraiture often encroach directly onto the portrait. Authors may feel that their manner of perception equals or even exceeds in importance the self which forms a text's ostensible subject, and they may divert considerable energy, both inside and outside the text, into exploring autobiographical aims and methods. Writers may do this for their own benefit or that of their readers; they may draw attention to aspects of methodology or attempt to disguise the rhetorical methods they have used. Yeats speculates repeatedly about the autobiographical process, and he frequently discusses such speculations within his autobiographical texts, so that his introspection becomes complex and cyclic, involving his methods of recollection, research and writing as well as the details of the recalled life itself.

Yeats, a public figure for much of his life, apparently felt no pressing need to conceal the mechanisms of autobiographical concealment. The supremacy of the artist's view could be taken for granted, the masks put on by the writer could be seen from all directions, and could even be discussed at length; the 'protagonist' of the sections of *Autobiographies* might become explicitly that, a figure created by Yeats whose creation the reader could watch. We cannot always distinguish autobiography from fiction in Yeats's texts, but his explicitness in describing his literary methods at least gives us the illusion of being able to do so.

Yeats's particular kind of self-consciousness led him to write constantly about himself, but he did not stop there. His inquisitive spirit and a desire for completeness led him to investigate the process of self-portrayal, and his letters, diaries and essays contain much speculation about autobiographical methodologies; so do his autobiographical writings themselves. He always maintained, in James Olney's terms, a point of view on his point of view.[2] Such cyclic introspection sometimes threatened to become narrowly reductive—or infinitely regressive—but Yeats usually escapes these traps through his sustained self-discipline, the use in autobiographical texts of private myths, metaphor, irony and humour, and the sheer restless fertility of his imagination, which never remained content for long with a single mode or theory of self-portraiture.

Yeats's autobiographical theory and practice both underwent continual evolution, partly as a response by one to Yeats's discoveries in the other. Sometimes one ran well in advance of the other. Speculation on methods might yield a text illustrating the methods, as happened with *The Trembling of the Veil*; or a completed work might prompt later investigation of the modes of self-analysis by which it had been composed, usually conducted in letters but occasionally in verse, as with his late re-evaluation of early autobiographical poetry and drama in 'The Circus Animals' Desertion'. Theory and practice—both of which are, especially for Yeats, at once creative and analytical acts—fed on and nourished one another.

Fastidious comparison of Yeats's autobiographical theory and practice, for the purpose of detecting inconsistencies, would therefore be a misguided and misguiding exercise. Discrepancies between the two are implicit in both, the theory sometimes attesting the difficulty of fulfilling its precepts, and the finished autobiographical texts sometimes admitting their own divergence from plans previously made for them. Theories devised after the fact are suspect too, having their own rhetorical purposes. Often Yeats deliberately avoided following his own prescriptions, or tried to change the meaning of his texts in retrospective analysis. The evolving relationship of precept and example throughout Yeats's autobiographical career thus offers an intriguing record of desired and feasible modes of self-presentation. Accidental—or deliberate—inconsistencies should not be pursued in an effort to find fault with Yeats, but taken as signs of particular difficulties caused by the nature of his personality or the kinds of writing he attempted.

Characteristically, Yeats began his autobiographical work with great caution, then in the reassuring presence of completed writing rapidly gained confidence in elaborating his ideas. Yet he found that much experimentation was necessary. Thus in October 1909, after several years of writing autobiographical poetry, he remarked that 'I am only just beginning to feel I can express myself' (*L* 536). The 1909 diary gave scope for speculations about his effects on the world and about possible ways of recording those effects; the survival of many of these speculations in the 1926-28 published versions presumably indicates that Yeats had accepted their validity throughout this time, besides revealing his wish to record this aspect of his earlier self. He also cultivated in the diary some of the autobiographical theories and methods he was later to transplant into *Reveries* and *The Trembling of the Veil*. In the construction of these texts (to change metaphors) such theories and methods became not only a blueprint but a kind of scaffolding which was to remain visible in the finished work; a statement of methods became part of the text, as a sign of good faith.

Yeats always needed an antagonist when testing his thoughts, and he tried out his musings about autobiographical writing on his father. In his correspondence with J. B. Yeats on the subject of personality, in 1910 and later, his ideas about self-portraiture can be seen maturing, and sometimes changing in response to his father's suggestions. In 1912 he advised his father to write his own autobiography: 'I suggest . . . that in your first chapter or chapters you describe old relations and your childhood. You have often told us most interesting things, pictures of old Ireland that should not be lost. . . . You could say anything about anything, for after all, you yourself would be the theme, there would be no need to be afraid of egotism' (*L* 571). Here Yeats gently contradicts his father's opinion, reported in *Reveries*, that personal utterance was 'only egotism' (*A* 102); he may also have been quietly clearing the way for easy paternal approval of his own autobiographical efforts. At the same time, Yeats's conception of autobiographical writing may have been refined and strengthened by exposure to his father's partly sceptical attitudes. Yeats continues his prescription for his father's imagined autobiography by suggesting 'probably, a good deal that you have written recently would fit in somewhere. The first chapter or two might be difficult, but after that, I know by experience of my own books that your thought would go on branching and blossoming in all directions' (*L* 572).

Yeats's prescription here implies that autobiographical writing should have documentary authenticity but also be impressionistic, should save the past from oblivion, and should mediate between the past and the present. He would not necessarily observe such rules himself, of course, particularly the rule that a writer should transcribe the past faithfully; indeed we might argue that by expounding the programme, ostensibly to assist his father, Yeats freed himself not to follow it. The programme may thus be as much a smokescreen as a map, and if so, Yeats's strategy here amusingly recalls the way in which he used his enthusiastic advocacy of the Gaelic-language revival as a means of avoiding actual study of the language; and, having decreed that we must choose to seek perfection in either life or work, proceeded to seek it in both. The prescription for autobiography is designed to fit his father's circumstances rather than his own; it also hints at an ulterior motive. Yeats wants to enlist his father as a research assistant, disclosing aspects of his own family background which Yeats would otherwise have had to unearth for himself. It was with a similar motive that, while working on *First Draft* in 1915, Yeats wrote to his father 'I would like from you any reveries or suggestions that occur to you' (*L* 603).

In 1913 Yeats included a crucial statement in another letter to his father: 'Of recent years instead of "vision", meaning by vision the intense realization of a state of ecstatic emotion symbolized in a definite imagined region, I have tried for more self portraiture' (*L* 583). It is not clear precisely what time-span Yeats has in mind here when he refers to 'recent years'; probably he implies changes which took place about 1910, but he might have dated the change back to the beginning of the century, when his poetry became much more naturalistically autobiographical than it had been previously. In any case, this is an example of the kind of retrospective application of theory which Yeats always enjoyed; by thus formulating a theoretical statement he gave shape to works already written and laid the foundations for new writing as well. The same process is visible in revisions to his poetry; his versatility and invention both rested partly on a constant re-evaluation of past work, so that he always knew, when embarking in a new direction, exactly what he was leaving behind. Yeats's emphasis on his quest for 'more self portraiture' suggests his desire to find in the self an adequate metaphysic as well as a theme. To treat the self in this way is to declare independence from any obligation to depict the external world faithfully. Autobiographical investigation and expression become one's primary forms of truth, and one can rest on the assumption that all the utterances of the passionate self must be true; Yeats conveys this assumption in many of his letters as well.

Yeats found the writing of *Reveries* straightforward enough: 'While I was immature I was a different person and I can stand apart and judge' (*L* 589). His beguilingly simple prefatory remarks in *Reveries* itself legitimate his desire for freedom to reconstruct the past as he now sees it or wants it to be seen, unencumbered by any conflicting recollections or evidence which other sources might seek to impose on him. That he wished his texts to display a harmony of form and content is implied in his 1922 discussion of Lady Gregory's memoirs, which in their concern with documentation are 'the reverse of my memoirs [here he refers to *The Trembling of the Veil*, but the remark applies equally well to *Reveries*] in every way, for I could not have quoted a letter or a diary without spoiling my effect' (*L* 684). The 'effect' he seeks, presumably, is not merely a smooth or didactic literary texture but the impression of a coherent, self-willed past.

As Yeats persevered with his autobiographical narrative past his safely distant childhood and youth, he became concerned that the existence of numerous witnesses to his recent years who were so unhelpful as to be still living might restrict his form as well as his content. In a 1914 letter to his father, already quoted, he says he has brought *Reveries* as far as 1886 or 1887, but feels that subsequently 'there would be too many living people to consider and [the texts] would have besides to be written in a different way. . . . I should always, I feel, write of other people. I dare say I shall return to the subject but only in fragments' (*L* 589). He hints here that the kind of truth he had sought in *Reveries* might be damaged by exposure to potentially hostile witnesses; omissions made necessary by this realisation would break up the texture of his prose. Yet he found ways to express personal truths even within such an impersonal and fragmented structure as he projects here, as he was also to do in *A Vision*, and may in fact have found the text engaging his personality at deeper levels than he had anticipated. While working on *The Trembling of the Veil* he remarked to Olivia Shakespear that 'I find this memoir writing makes me feel clean, as if I had bathed and put on clean linen. It rids me of something and I shall return to poetry with a renewed simplicity' (*L* 672). Thus autobiographical writing should have a cathartic function; and it becomes a way of purifying and strengthening the relation between the poet and the imaginative work. This programme again anticipates *A Vision*. Yeats claims to have achieved detachment, insisting that while he studies others at moments of crisis, he lacks a crisis himself. Here he begins, perhaps unconsciously, to speak of his work as a fiction; the sexual, intellectual and other 'crises' which beset him in the 1890s have been quietly edited out of his autobiographical writings and, equally, out of his comments on them. In this way he approaches Gide's method of attempting to change the shape of his actual past by retroactive decree. To omit an incident from his autobiographical writings was, by implication, to reduce its significance in his memory as well.

Yeats found that this kind of editing became more difficult as he brought his autobiography towards the present, presumably because so much was already known about his life. In 1926 he remarked to Olivia Shakespear: 'My new Autobiography—1900 to 1926—may be the final test of my intellect, my last great effort, and I keep putting it off' (*L* 721). At this time, Yeats was already directing much of his energy into consistently autobiographical poetry, where he could escape from the adherence to sequence and logical causality demanded by prose, and express himself more tersely and enigmatically. He had probably come to feel that this poetry expressed his life more adequately than anything prose could achieve. Certainly, the poetry fed on perceptions developed during the writing of *The Trembling of the*

Veil.[3] Yeats never did write the 'new Autobiography' in the form he said he had once envisaged it, and the more straightforward, less imaginative passages (letters, diaries, an expository essay and a speech) with which he filled out *Autobiographies* drew from him little theoretical or interpretive comment either before or after publication, though they do serve to illustrate his continuing dissatisfaction with purely narrative forms of self-presentation. His interest in discursive autobiographical writing seems to have waned considerably after the late 1920s.

Yeats's purposes in writing different parts of *Autobiographies* vary, as does his candour in acknowledging these purposes. Sometimes he seems to avow a real but minor concern while skipping past more important preoccupations. Thus in *The Trembling of the Veil* his accounts of other people are intended to illuminate his own personality—especially his stability and integrity, contrasting with the waywardness and disintegration of the unsuccessful, self-destructive figures around him—much more emphatically than he ever admits, yet in fact serve to make it still more puzzling. Real detachment in an account of one's past may, indeed, require the inclusion of a more specific representation of the self than Yeats chooses to provide. The presence of such a self-representation may actually conceal the complexities of selfhood more completely than would its absence, since it permits direct authorial control over a reader's perceptions of the author. Yeats's reluctance to appear makes us wonder where he is hiding. Often Yeats gives an altruistic, socially concerned motive for writing: his work will serve future generations of Irish students (here he follows, at least in theory, the prescription which he had supplied to his father), the poet's life has instructive value for others, the achievements of Synge and Lady Gregory must be made known, and their detractors denounced, in a context where Yeats's own indebtedness to and respect for them can be made manifest. He claims that the purpose of the literary personality he constructs for himself is to 'oppose the new ill-breeding of Ireland' (*A* 463).

Yeats's detachment led him to study 'personality' chiefly in the area he most thoroughly understood; his self-preoccupation always owed more to integrity than to egotism. He often aims to satisfy his own curiosity or to establish 'metaphors for poetry', yet he makes public property of the results of his quest. In *Per*

Amica Silentia Lunae he remarks 'When I remember that Shelley calls our minds "mirrors of the fire for which all thirst", I cannot but ask the question all have asked, "What or who has cracked the mirror?" I begin to study the only self that I can know, myself, and to wind the thread upon the pern again' (*MY* 364). In 'Four Years', Yeats implies that self-knowledge confers an obligation to project onto the world an image of the self (*A* 143); in 'Ireland after Parnell' he seems to regard power over self and expression of self as equivalent (*A* 233).

Yeats admits in *Estrangement* his wish to provide a consistent and substantial image of the poet behind the poems: 'Whatever happens I must go on that there may be a man behind the lines already written; I cast the die long ago and must be true to the cast' (*A* 485).[4] In this way the autobiography will serve partly as a critical apparatus, informing a reading of the poems and plays, if only by presenting an image of the poet complementing that given in his ostensibly more imaginative writing. He probably wants his readers to regard the autobiography as a repository of facts from which the poetry can take off on its imaginative flights, the role which *A Vision* was also to serve; this assumption would be, of course, a considerable simplification. Often, though, Yeats warns of more speculative purposes. He has had to make a tradition for and of himself: 'Lacking sufficient recognized precedent, I must needs find out some reason for all I did' (*A* 166). In *The Death of Synge* Yeats acknowledges that 'I write for my own good' (*A* 502); though he does not hint, as do some autobiographers, that this therapeutic purpose in itself suffices to establish literary merit, and he mostly subdues his references to this function in preparing his diary for publication. The confession that he writes for his own good had been more explicit and positive in the diary; as he says there, he is sure that he has made moral gains (*M* 190). But Yeats's magniloquent and declamatory style—in *Autobiographies* he usually writes as if to prevent an imagined antagonist from getting a word in—threatens to hide such confessions that private investigations for private ends may be involved, and seems intended to have such an effect. Yeats appears intent on converting the multiplicity of the world into unity, and one sometimes forgets that he also wishes to perform the same task in terms of his own character. His aims may, indeed, have always been more private and therapeutic than he normally allowed his comments to admit or his style to imply.

Although he never seems to have worried much about the limits of self-knowledge or the risk of forgetting the past, Yeats had mixed feelings about the technical feasibility of self-portraiture. 'We are never a unity, a personality to ourselves', he reflects (*A* 503). Even his diary oscillates markedly between impulses to concealment and to revelation, between an implied private audience and a more public one. *First Draft* was not for publication in Yeats's lifetime, 'if ever'; even so, he felt compelled in it to change such details as Olivia Shakespear's name (we wonder whether he made this alteration through fear that his text might fall into the wrong hands or because he found it easier to write about Olivia Shakespear's role in his life in partly fictitious terms). His desire to confess warred continually with his shyness. Moreover, his genuinely good-natured attitude to most of the people he had to discuss (with a few obvious exceptions, such as George Moore—and he waited until Moore died before writing about him) forced on him an often attractive but also potentially distorting reticence. *First Draft* shows struggles with his father considerably more intense and painful than the tensions which he allowed to appear in *Reveries*: with apt irony and premonitory symbolism, Yeats begins *First Draft* by recounting an incident in which his father smashed the glass of a framed picture with the back of Yeats's head. On the other hand, Ronsley notes that in *Reveries* Yeats, talking of a play which he had written to express his frustration at his father's influence on him, modified the plot to purge it of critical overtones.[5]

Yeats was never able or willing to paint a 'definitive' portrait of even part of his life, though he approached such an achievement in *Reveries*. Consequently, he risks the kind of distortion which his father created in a painting, mentioned already in Chapter 7, by superimposing the seasonal variations of a landscape on a single canvas until snow obliterated the details of previous seasons. Whether Yeats intended the implication or not, his account of this incident (*A* 28) applies as eloquently to dangers inherent in his own personality and methods as to the limitations he perceived in his father; a perfectionism which began with the laudable desire to represent life as accurately as possible may end, paradoxically, by imposing on it a deathly, monochromatic stasis. Yeats's writing constantly juxtaposes a desire for definition and completeness with the realisation that life prohibits such finality. In *Estrangement* he reflects that 'neither Christ nor Buddha nor Socrates wrote a book, for to do that is to exchange life for a logical process' (*A* 461). To summarise part of a life may be to detach and even remove it from the rest of the life, and so to lose any inspiration it might have provided. Yeats jealously guards the sacredness of his own past.

He sometimes doubted the feasibility of significant autobiographical writing so radically that he almost repudiated the notion. In his last letter to have been published he implies that conventional self-depiction, with its inevitable stress on detail and contingency, has long ceased to satisfy his desire for unity: 'When I try to put all into a phrase I say, "Man can embody truth but he cannot know it". I must embody it in the completion of my life' (*L* 922). In retrospect even an autobiography may become merely a part of the debris of existence, and thus an inadequate expression of the life's essence, which can appear truly only in the life itself as it approaches culmination. The superb evocation of human transience with which Nabokov begins *Speak, Memory* qualifies the rest of the autobiography and so makes a similar point more dramatically: 'The cradle rocks above an abyss, and common sense tells us that our existence is but a brief crack of light between two eternities of darkness'.[6] Yet Nabokov still finds ways to exploit his acute awareness of the transience of naturalistic experience in order to lend a compensatory and lasting validity to his reaction to that experience. Yeats, too, sometimes saw the permanence of art (presumably including autobiographical art) as a compensation for the evanescence of life. C. G. Jung has eloquently expressed fears resembling those sometimes voiced by Yeats:

> I myself have a distaste for autobiography. The immense expanse of possibly recognizable objects in the world has lured me forth to those twilit border zones where the figure I have meanwhile become steps towards me. . . . He who mounts a flight of steps does not linger on them, nor look

back at them, even though age invites him to linger or slow down his pace. The great wind of the peaks roars ever more loudly in his ears. His gaze sweeps distances that flee away into the infinite. The last steps are the loveliest and most precious, for they lead to that fullness to reach which the innermost essence of man is born.[7]

Jung's sentiments and images here seem curiously to fuse the spirits of Nabokov, Ibsen and Goethe; not that imaginative writers generally, and certainly not a fastidious one like Yeats, would approve of the partial surrender of personality Jung seems to contemplate. But Yeats would undoubtedly have agreed with Jung's implication that the deepest sense of the reality of a life is incommunicable, capable of achievement only within the life itself and not to be transferred to an account of it. In 'The Autumn of the Body' Yeats reflects that even in terms of inner experience, those parts of a life which are susceptible to autobiographical treatment appear trivial beside deeper, more mysterious realities: 'Our thoughts and emotions are often but spray flung up from hidden tides that follow a moon no eye can see' (*E&I* 189).

Yeats usually felt able to reach agreement with such doubts, and his urge to build a coherent mythology of self made him persevere despite them. Yet his sensitivity to the hazards and limitations of self-portraiture led him directly to another paradox. The candour which autobiographical investigation seems to demand may be threatened by the desire to control images of the self; yet a candid account of one's own process of self-analysis, a process without which one could obviously not write autobiographically at all, requires in turn that such images should be diligently watched and reinforced. Any self-consciousness imposes such a paradox, but in Yeats's case it is exacerbated by deeply-held convictions about art and life. He felt that to be seen as sincere and credible, he must make great efforts of self-control, and create, in effect, a distinct public persona. Candour may be better served by building up the self than by anatomising it. Yeats insists on the necessary self-discipline of assuming a second self (*A* 469); and in his letter discussing his aim of closer self-portraiture he insists that 'I have tried to make my work convincing with a speech so natural and dramatic that the hearer would feel the presence of a man thinking and feeling' (*L* 583). Thus a created self is to be more 'real' than the real self.

This emphasis accords with Yeats's constantly idiosyncratic use of the term 'reality', and it cannot be dismissed as a quibble. If reality resides in what one has created rather than in the raw material from which that creation is made, any analysis of the 'given', uncreated self is in danger of becoming reductive and disguising what is felt to be the true essence of the personality: self-creation. In his 1910 lecture 'Friends of My Youth' Yeats remarks that a poet's life 'is an experiment in living and those that come after have a right to know it';[8] to know it, that is, in the form which the poet has deliberately given to it. Thus Yeats argues that through their 'experiment in living', imaginative artists create a self as they create their work, and that their work cannot be appreciated without an understanding of this created self. This is a more sophisticated (and in some ways more accurate) version of his remarks on the need to convey a sense of the actual self behind his poems.

A danger appears here, in that such assumptions may provide an excuse for merely quizzical analyses of one's own habit of posing. (Yeats did occasionally lapse into this rather precious kind of analysis in his diary, but edited more self-indulgent passages out of his published text.) If the self to be analysed is not the 'given' self but a deliberate creation, and if both the creation and modes of investigating it can change constantly, then the possibilities for fussy self-scrutiny may be multiplied almost indefinitely. The attempt to separate the perceived self from the perceiving, to make it an object, cannot be altogether successful when the whole self (and not merely an aspect of it) is involved. Coleridge, in his account of self-consciousness as the eternal I AM, stresses the fusion of the self and images of the self; in a self-conscious being, 'object and subject, being and knowing, are identical, each involving and supposing the other'; the subject 'becomes a subject by the act of constructing itself objectively to itself'.[9] Nevertheless, most autobiographers do write of a self differing at least slightly from their true past identity—the very act of recall changes the facts recalled—and to this extent all autobiographical writing treats a partly fictional self.

Yet in Yeats the recorded self is consciously and frequently changed to accord with each new impulse towards revelation or concealment. He acknowledges in 'A General Introduction for My Work' that the poet—and hence, we may assume, the imaginative autobiographer—heightens the material of actual life when presenting it: 'A poet writes always of his personal life, in his finest work out of its tragedy, whatever it be, remorse, lost love, or mere loneliness [this supposedly general pronouncement has obvious and deep roots in Yeats's own experience]; he never speaks directly as to someone at the breakfast table, there is always a phantasmagoria' (*E&I* 509). The poet 'has been reborn as an idea, something intended, complete'. Yeats thus justifies the mode of imaginative recreation of experience which he practises frequently in his poetry and in *Autobiographies*.

Some readers, becoming aware of this blatant (if confessed) authorial manipulation, may be led to doubt Yeats's sincerity. Certainly a witty, evasive and sometimes disdainful tone pervades much of *Autobiographies*; Yeats gives away very little, if anything, involuntarily, and what he chooses to tell he filters and controls with great care. The observation that the selectivity or evasiveness of the autobiographer in itself makes a kind of autobiographical statement, though doubtless true, does not help much in this case; as long as mixed motives cause excisions from the text we cannot be certain that the result takes the form Yeats would have preferred, and the engaging frankness of *First Draft* may, despite appearances, more accurately represent his ideal form of autobiographical writing (his poetry moves progressively towards frankness through his career). Yet he establishes his own form of sincerity, which for him consists less in uninhibited self-revelation (which would be a distortion of his personality, hence insincere) than in a strict fidelity to evolving artistic preoccupations.

The result in Yeats's text, though, remains remarkably fluid, as the use of masks produces a recording autobiographer who changes as continually and as dramatically as his recorded self. George Russell observes that Yeats 'began about the time of *The Wind among the Reeds* to do two things consciously, one to create a "style" in literature, the second to create or rather re-create W. B. Yeats in a style which would harmonize with the literary style'.[10] Thus Yeats creates both a past self, a distillation and transmutation of his actual past, and a present self, similarly composed of aspects of his present personality, with which to record the past. The past self is created partly by a process of divining what the present self is not (or has ceased to be); but awareness of this discrepancy may, perversely, make the two selves grow more nearly akin. Yeats's method creates a constant flickering between creative and created selves, a kind of alternating current, which nevertheless produces in the reader the illusion of a steady flow of investigative energy from present to past. Perloff remarks that 'present' Yeats claims superiority to 'past' Yeats by his ability to judge Maud Gonne objectively, but in fact fails to achieve this degree of detachment.[11]

Yeats will only seem sincere if we accept his view that truth to art, for him a necessary part of his integrity, requires rigorous selection even in the most immediate of personal statements. What will help to convince us is Yeats's belief, stressed throughout *Autobiographies*, that his peculiar personality forced him irrevocably to the assumption of a mask. His youthful sense of isolation and weakness, described in *Reveries*, is presented as a further justification for the use of such a shield. In this sense, self-awareness becomes cyclic: the past which Yeats describes both produces and grows out of the aesthetic assumptions informing its creation. Just how difficult Yeats felt the problems of self-interpretation and self-disclosure to be appears in a crucial and attractive passage in *Per Amica Silentia Lunae*, where he discusses the creative and created selves. Yeats confesses that—at times—'I am in the place where the Daimon is, but I do not think he is with me until I begin to make a new personality, selecting among . . . images, seeking always to satisfy a hunger grown out of conceit with daily diet; and yet as I write the words "I select", I am full of uncertainty, not knowing when I am the finger, when the clay' (*MY* 365–6). In writing autobiographically one faces the constant perplexity of being both the finger and the clay, and of knowing that such is the case. The tension described here resembles that between tenor and vehicle, or between Self and Anti-self in terms of Yeats's System.

Yeats nonetheless felt that life and art should be founded on the dynamic relationship between actual self and created anti-self, a relationship which served partly as a means of controlling external tensions by internalising them. He had a persistent inclination to find symbolism in both present and past, a tendency which led him away from the literal, objective significance of experiences and memories yet held him back from a purely fanciful realm where he might elude the correspondences which symbolism demands. In Yeats's world the ostensibly antithetical or disparate processes by which art becomes life and life becomes art are made curiously interchangeable; Michael Robartes becomes as real as Maud Gonne, while Mr Yeats becomes a confessedly fictional character, as in 'The Phases of the Moon', about whom his created personae dutifully write. As Ronsley remarks, 'the artist's life and its expression are mutually inadequate. Only by their being brought together in his symbolic imagination can either life or art have meaning or project truth'.[12] For Yeats, life and art must become not identical but reciprocal, each expressing the other. 'There is in Yeats's case', as Jacqueline Genet points out, 'not a straightforward relationship between life and work, but a true interaction'.[13]

Yeats occasionally discusses in detail his methods of creating his autobiography. He talks about his alternating exploitation or deliberate neglect of documentation and about various ways of controlling self-consciousness by the precise apprehension and delineation of the material under discussion in an autobiographical passage. He mentions in letters his attempt to achieve balance in his portrait of George Moore by re-reading most of Moore's work before he began writing; though he does not admit, as must have been the case, that he was also looking for material to use against Moore. (He also says that he hated reading Moore.) Although he had insisted on his right to quote his father's conversation without permission in *Reveries*, for *The Trembling of the Veil* he claimed to achieve impartiality by allowing those he discussed to check his work before publication. Thus he wrote to George Russell: 'I will submit to you whatever I write about yourself and publish nothing that you dislike. I wish to be able to say in my preface that wherever I have included a living man I have submitted my words for his correction' (*L* 670). This remark sounds a little disingenuous, partly because Yeats made free with information about those of his subjects who were now dead, as most were; and partly, too, because he places such heavy emphasis on his wish to justify and provide that prefatory claim of decorum and authenticity. Also, by submitting to particular readers only those portions of the text most directly applicable to them, Yeats retained control of his work's general plan (and, clearly, he attached great importance to the rhetorical integrity of the book); if a reader requested a particular change in the text, Yeats could easily compensate for it elsewhere if he so wished. Thus he retains considerably more control than he admits.

Despite his remark that his father 'could say anything about anything' in his autobiography, Yeats always appreciated that in any autobiographical writing selection and shaping take precedence over fact and documentation, that the autobiographer presents a created rather than a remembered self. He never believed that autobiographical writing could be fully impartial or factual, or even that such a goal was desirable. His remark that when he was immature he was a different person, whom he could now judge as if from a distance, confirms his awareness of the need for conscious and imaginative evaluation. If his inclination to treat his life as fiction is not always explicitly acknowledged, his tendency to dramatise it is, if anything, exaggerated; metaphors drawn from drama and the theatre pervade *The Trembling of the Veil* and, especially, *Dramatis Personae*, and it is clear that Yeats intends these metaphors to apply to his manner of self-presentation. The multiple implications of the title *Dramatis Personae* neatly reflect his sense of the life-and-art duality. Donoghue remarks that in *First Draft*, ancestor of *The Trembling of the Veil* and part of *Dramatis Personae*, Yeats 'moves from one person to another, handing each a script, his part in the play. He does not merely enumerate the events of a plot: behind the several scripts, he composes a generation, many lives engaged in a play of history' (*M* 10).

Yeats should accept the validity of this comparison of his autobiographical theory and practice. He has his own theory about theories, and in *Ideas of Good and Evil* he discusses the need for poets to develop a clear sense of purpose before composing. He tests the work of Blake against his own assumptions about Blake's ideas and attitudes. Moreover, Yeats often provokes comparison by placing theoretical remarks within other writings, so that *Autobiographies*, for example, becomes a work about its own presuppositions and creation as much as about its writer.

Such fusions and clashes of precept and example have a metaphysical basis, apart from the function they serve in dramatising the problems of composition. Yeats constantly joins a record of the contingencies of life with an ideal of how life should be recorded, and hence—given his belief in the power of art to shape life—of how it should be lived in consonance with (though not subjection to) aesthetic criteria. He thus maintains his balance between fact and fantasy, controlling life's dualities by providing both an image and an idea, both a dancer and a dance. Perhaps he ultimately asserts control by attempting to fuse all dualities into a single duality; this is a possible interpretation of his gyre symbol. Theory and practice meet in that vital nucleus of the Yeatsian universe, the arena where dreams become responsibility and where responsibility gives way in turn to dreams. It is thus no coincidence that the interplay of his precepts and examples so often seems to take us near the energising centre of his constantly shifting thought. This interplay tells us more about Yeats than either theory or practice studied alone.

Yet—to give Yeats the last word on the matter, something which he works hard to gain—the theory functions partly as a decoy. At any point in its evolution it possesses its own remarkable consistency and imaginative quality, and Yeats deliberately blurs distinctions between it and his practice. Ingeniously, he thus leaves his practice free to take its own road, and to indulge in subtleties of which the theory can profess a blissful ignorance. Such deft manipulation allows him to exercise in autobiographical writing that high degree of literary control which he found so necessary, and so fruitful, throughout his work.

Yeats was a dedicated artist who wrote constantly about himself. Autobiographical modes were of continuing vital importance to him, and his power to manipulate these modes became a cherished possession. Always introspective, he characteristically chose to discuss his methodology expansively in an attempt to avoid misinterpretation and to keep control at all points.

Yeats said that the human intellect must choose perfection in either life or work, but having prescribed the choice he refrained from making it, and strove for perfection in both realms. As a result his autobiographical work attains remarkable intricacy. His autobiographical impulses may also have helped to dictate the genres in which he concentrated his imaginative work. He found his natural voice—lyric poetry— early, and used it for his most satisfactory autobiographical performances, supplementing it with the plays which helped him to overcome his reticence; novels and memoirs, and in the end even *Autobiographies* itself, failed to satisfy his desire to convey his character in definitive lineaments rather than through elaborate discourse. Always there remained in his real life something irreducible, which would resist satisfactory transformation into any literary medium.

Yeats appreciated that autobiographical expression is a universal phenomenon, reaching its highest possibilities in the work of imaginative authors, but common to everyone. Aristocratically, he argues that possessing a sense of one's past produces greater psychological coherence, hence more concentrated self-expression and an ability to assert one's superiority. Listening to Yeats, we always know who is talking; Yeats's characters only sound convincing when they sound like Yeats. Autobiographical activity certainly helped him to acquire that distinctive voice.

He also sensed keenly the fascination which most readers feel with the lives of writers. In *The Trembling of the Veil* Yeats notes that 'I took great pleasure in certain allusions to the singer's life one finds in old romances and ballads, and thought his presence there all the more poignant because we discover it half lost, like portly Chaucer, behind his own maunciple and pardoner upon the Canterbury roads' (*A* 151). This is to invite us to find Yeats behind his work as well. Nabokov reminds us:

A poet's life resembles a parody of his work. The passage of time, it seems, seeks to re-enact the gesture of the genius by giving his imaginative existence the same colour and shape as the poet had given to his creatures. What does it matter, finally, if what we see is no more than a vast pretence? It still gives a degree of pleasure which the sharpest criticism— even that which I direct at myself—cannot destroy.[14]

Because Yeats concentrates so persistently on the material of his own life when constructing imaginative works, he inevitably speculates on the ways in which readers will perceive that life. Then he writes autobiographical texts which seek to shape his reader's responses. He aims to make explicit and incontrovertible his multiple attempts to fuse his life into unity—or at least to give us the impression that this is what he has done. He retains to the last a lively awareness of the complex interplay of his actual life, his imaginative accounts of his life, and his readers' responses to these accounts. The subtlety of these perceptions, and his courage and rigour in exploring such relationships from many points of view, give his work much of its fascination.

Notes

Chapter 1
Thinking about Autobiography
pp. 1–11
1. Too much material of this kind now exists to permit a point-by-point discussion involving the work of many critics. Several essays on the subject have been collected by James Olney in his useful anthology *Autobiography: Essays Theoretical and Critical*, which also contains a bibliography of further writings about autobiography. Particularly helpful accounts have also been written by Francis R. Hart ('Notes for an Anatomy of Modern Autobiography') and Elizabeth W. Bruss (*Autobiographical Acts: The Changing Situation of a Literary Genre*).
2. Bruss, *Autobiographical Acts*, 18.
3. David Goldknopf, *The Life of the Novel*, 60.
4. Vladimir Nabokov, *Strong Opinions*, 18.
5. T. S. Eliot, 'The Dry Salvages', in *The Complete Poems and Plays of T. S. Eliot*, 186.
6. Eliot, 'East Coker', *Complete Poems and Plays*, 179.
7. Eliot, *Complete Poems and Plays*, 293.
8. Robert Scholes and Robert Kellogg, *The Nature of Narrative*, 157.
9. See André Gide, *Si le grain ne meurt*, 281; translation by present author.
10. See *A* 113, 558.

Chapter 2
Autobiographical Fiction
pp. 12–34
1. Some of the material in this chapter has appeared previously in my article 'Yeats as a Novelist', *Journal of Modern Literature*, 12 (1985), 261–76, copyright Temple University. I am grateful for permission to draw on this material here.
2. See Richard J. Finneran's Introduction to his edition, *JS* 25.
3. See William M. Murphy, 'William Butler Yeats's *John Sherman*: An Irish Poet's Declaration of Independence', 97–8.
4. See Denis Donoghue's note, *M* 32, and Murphy, 'William Butler Yeats's *John Sherman*', 100–101.
5. An amusing gloss on the chess-playing in *John Sherman* appears in William M. Murphy's *Prodigal Father*. Murphy records that Yeats sometimes played chess against himself; also that he played it against his father but always lost. 'The son could see the sweep and flow of the wooden armies as they advanced in beautiful ranks against each other, but he tended to overlook bishops that were about to be captured by knights' (Murphy, *Prodigal Father*, 131).

6. In this chapter the title *The Speckled Bird* will be used primarily to refer to the 'Final' version of the text except where the context makes clear that all four versions are meant.

7. Ann Fallon suggests a further association with St. John the Apostle; see 'Toward the Internalization of the Myth', 122–3.

8. See William H. O'Donnell's speculations on this subject, *SB* li–lii. Maud Gonne's marriage may be yet another reason for Yeats's abandoning the novel.

9. See William H. O'Donnell, 'Yeats as Adept and Artist', in G. M. Harper, ed., *Yeats and the Occult*, 55–79.

10. Warwick Gould, '"Lionel Johnson Comes the First to Mind": Sources for Owen Aherne', in Harper, *Yeats and the Occult*, 255–84.

11. In Harper, *Yeats and the Occult*, 269.

12. Michael J. Sidnell, 'Mr Yeats, Michael Robartes, and Their Circle', in Harper, *Yeats and the Occult*, 252–3.

Chapter 3
Reveries over Childhood and Youth
pp. 35–45

1. These shared features do not all prove Yeatsian borrowing, however. Yeats could not have seen the end of the *Portrait* when he wrote *Reveries*. There are also interesting resemblances between the *Portrait* and *The Trembling of the Veil*; see Chapter 4 below.

2. Marjorie Perloff, 'The Tradition of Myself', 540.

3. Perloff, 539.

4. Joseph Ronsley, *Yeats's Autobiography*, 34.

5. In a typescript passage which Yeats excised before publication he associates with his Middleton relations a tradition that 'the plaster cracks in the generation after a peasant marriage'. See Curtis Bradford, *Yeats at Work*, 346.

Chapter 4
The Trembling of the Veil
pp. 46–61

1. Yeats may have had in mind the structure of a five-act play rather than that of Joyce's novel.

2. Published in 1972 by Donoghue in *Memoirs*.

3. Daniel T. O'Hara, *Tragic Knowledge*, 123.

4. Compare Yeats's treatment of the Easter Rising ('Easter 1916') and the Irish Civil War ('Meditations in Time of Civil War'); in both cases he emphasises the dramatic, playlike connotations of these events.

Chapter 5
Dramatis Personae
pp. 62–74

1. See Ronsley, *Yeats's Autobiography*, 119.

Chapter 6
Estrangement and *The Death of Synge*
pp. 75–82
1. Ronsley, *Yeats's Autobiography*, 11.

Chapter 7
The Bounty of Sweden
pp. 83–8
1. Shirley Neuman, *Some One Myth*, 114.
2. Ronsley, *Yeats's Autobiography*, 129.

Chapter 8
Behind the Lines
pp. 89–107
1. Some of the material in this chapter has appeared previously in my article 'Behind the Lines: Strategies of Self-Portraiture in Yeats and Joyce', *Colby Library Quarterly*, 16 (1980), 148–57. I am grateful for permission to draw on this material here.
2. James Olney, *Metaphors of Self*, 43.
3. See Perloff, 'The Tradition of Myself'.
4. In the diary the last phrase in this sentence had read 'I should have avoided the thing—but being in it!' (*M* 172). The published version thus sounds considerably more committed.
5. Ronsley, *Yeats's Autobiography*, 43.
6. Nabokov, *Speak, Memory*, 19.
7. Quoted by Olney in *Metaphors of Self*, 149–50.
8. Quoted by Ronsley in *Yeats's Autobiography*, 2.
9. S. T. Coleridge, *Biographia Literaria*, *I*, 273.
10. Quoted by Ronsley in *Yeats's Autobiography*, 2.
11. See Perloff, 'The Tradition of Myself', 551. Richard Poirier, speaking of Norman Mailer, argues that the recorded impressions of both past and present selves are distorted by particular historical circumstances, and that discrepancies between these two sets of circumstances generate a third persona which tries to mediate between them. This 'third Mailer' hypothesis seems unnecessarily complex. It is the present self, however beset by its own circumstances, which mediates with the past self. See Poirier, *The Performing Self*, 16.
12. Ronsley, *Yeats's Autobiography*, 2–3.
13. Jacqueline Genet, *William Butler Yeats*, 17; translation by present author.
14. Nabokov, 'Pouchkine, ou le vrai et le vraisemblable', 367; translation by present author.

Appendix

Passages from *Journal* published in *Estrangement* and *The Death of Synge*
(See Donoghue, *M* 303):

Journal	*Estrangement*	*Journal*	*Estrangement*
4	II	50	XXVIII
5	I	51	XXIX, XXXIV
6	III	53	XXIX
9	IV	54	XXIX
11	V	55	XXXV
14	VI	56	XXX
16	VII	58	XXX
18	VIII	59	XXXI
19	IX	60	XXXII
20	X	61	XXXIII
21	X	64	LIV
22	XI	65	XXXVI
24	XII	68	XXXVII
25	XIII	71	XXXVIII
26	XIV	74	XXXIX
27	XV	75	XL
28	XVI	76	XLI
29	XVII	78	XLII
30	XVIII	79	XLIII
31	XIX	80	XLIV
32	XX	81	XLV
33	XXI	82	XLVI
34	XXII	83	XLVII
35	XXIII	84	XLVIII
36	XXIV	85	XLIX
38	XXV	87	L
39	XXV	88	LI
42	XXV	93	LII
46	XXVI	94	LIII
47	XXVII	95	LV

Journal	The Death of Synge		Journal	The Death of Synge
97	I		137	XX
98	II		138	XXI
99	III		140	XXI
100	IV		141	XXII
101	IV		143	XXIII
102	IV		144	XXIII
105	V		145	XXIV
107	VI		147	XXV
108	VII		150	XXVI
109	VIII		152	XXVII
114	IX		153	XXVIII
116	X		154	XXVII
117	XI		156	XXIX
118	XII		173	XXX
119	XIII		178	XXXI
120	XIV		191	XXXII
122	XV		192	XXXIII
123	XVI		194	XXXIV, XXXV
126	XVI		195	XXXVI
127	XVI		203	XXXVII
128	XVII		204	XXXVIII
129	XVIII		231	XXXIX
130	XVIII		233	XL
131	XIX		246	XLI
134	XX			

Writing and Publication History of *Autobiographies* and Related Texts

Title	Composition and Development	Surviving MSS., TSS.	Publication
'Verlaine in 1894'	Written ?1896; later became part of 'The Tragic Generation' in *The Trembling of the Veil*, 1922.	—	*The Savoy*, April 1896.
'The Folly of Argument'	Written Dec. 1908–March 1909. Chs. II, I, III taken from diary; later became parts I, II, V in *Estrangement*, 1926. (One section of the diary appeared as 'Synge' in the *English Review*, March 1913, and two in *Per Amica Silentia Lunae*, dated 1917.)	See entry below for *Journal*.	*The Manchester Playgoer*, June 1911.
Reveries over Childhood and Youth	Written Jan.-Dec. 1914. Appeared, modified, in *Autobiographies*, 1926.	'Corrected partial' TS., Dublin. MS. and two other TSS. lost? (Bradford 337–8.)	Cuala Press, March 1916 (*B* 111); Macmillan (N. Y.), April 1916 (*B* 112); Macmillan (London), Oct. 1916 (*B* 113).
'Four Years' and *Four Years*	Written 1920-June 1921. Partly based on *First Draft*. Appeared, much modified, in *The Trembling of the Veil*, 1922.	Two complete MSS., the second being close to the Cuala Press text (Bradford 351)	*The London Mercury* and *The Dial*, June-August 1921. Cuala Press, Dec. 1921 (*B* 131)
'More Memories'	Written ?1921-May 1922. Partly based on *First Draft*. Contained material which later formed the bulk of *The Trembling of the Veil*.	Nearly complete MS. of 'Ireland after Parnell'; principal MS. fragments (Bradford 356)	*The London Mercury*, May-Aug. 1922. *The Dial*, May-Oct. 1922.

Title	Composition and Development	Surviving MSS., TSS.	Publication
The Trembling of the Veil	Mostly already written; 'Four Years' extensively revised; material added elsewhere, including all of 'The Stirring of the Bones'.	MSS. and TSS. of Yeats's revisions to 'Four Years' survive (Bradford 356)	T. Werner Laurie, Oct. 1922 (*B* 133).
'A Biographical Fragment, with Some Notes'	Written ?1923. Closely based on *First Draft*. Became part of *The Trembling of the Veil* in *A*, 1926.	No known MS. (Bradford 372)	*The Criterion* and *The Dial*, July 1923.
The Bounty of Sweden	Written 1924. Became part of *Dramatis Personae*, 1926. Included 'The Irish Dramatic Movement'.	MS. of *The Bounty of Sweden* exists; apparently none for 'The Irish Dramatic Movement'.	*The London Mercury* and *The Dial*, Sept. 1924. Cuala Press, July 1925 (*B* 146)
Estrangement	Part of diary for Dec. 1908-March 1909; 61 of 95 entries used.	See entry below for *Journal*	Cuala Press, Aug. 1926 (*B* 150). *The London Mercury*, Oct.-Nov. 1926. *The Dial*, Nov. 1926.
Autobiographies	Included *Reveries over Childhood and Youth*, revised; *The Trembling of the Veil*, enlarged and revised; 'A Biographical Fragment' added.	—	Macmillan (London), Nov. 1926 (*B* 151); Macmillan (N. Y.), Feb. 1927 (*B* 152).
The Death of Synge	Part of diary for March 1909-Oct. 1914; 50 of 149 entries used.	See entry below for *Journal*	*The London Mercury* and *The Dial*, April 1928. Cuala Press, June 1928 (*B* 162).

Title	Composition and Development	Surviving MSS., TSS.	Publication
Dramatis Personae	Written 1934. Partly based on *First Draft*. Originally to be called 'Lady Gregory'.	Early MSS. lost? Late MS. and a TS. exist.	*The London Mercury*, Nov. 1935-Jan. 1936. Cuala Press, Dec. 1935 (*B* 183). *The New Republic*, Feb.-April 1936.
Dramatis Personae	Included the earlier *Dramatis Personae*, *Estrangement*, *The Death of Synge*, *The Bounty of Sweden*. Slight revisions.	—	Macmillan (N. Y.), May 1936 (*B* 186). Macmillan (London), May 1936 (*B* 187).
The Autobiography	Combined contents of *Autobiographies* (1926) and *Dramatis Personae* (1936). 'The Irish Dramatic Movement' omitted.	—	Macmillan (N. Y.), Aug. 1938 (*B* 198). Reissued 1953 (*B* 211G).
'Pages from a Diary Written in 1930'	Part of diary for April-Nov. 1930.	See entry below for *Journal*.	Cuala Press, Nov. 1944 (*B* 207).
Autobiographies	Contents as in *The Autobiography* (1938); 'The Irish Dramatic Movement' restored.	—	Macmillan (London), March 1955 (*B* 211L).
Reflections, ed. Bradford	Diary entries for April 1909-Oct. 1914 *not* used by Yeats in *The Death of Synge* now published separately.	See entry below for *Journal*	Cuala Press, 1970.
Memoirs, ed. Donoghue	*First Draft* and diary for 1908-30 published in full, the diary as *Journal*. *First Draft* written in 1915-17.	MSS. of *First Draft* and *Journal* exist in full (Bradford 337)	Macmillan (London), 1972.

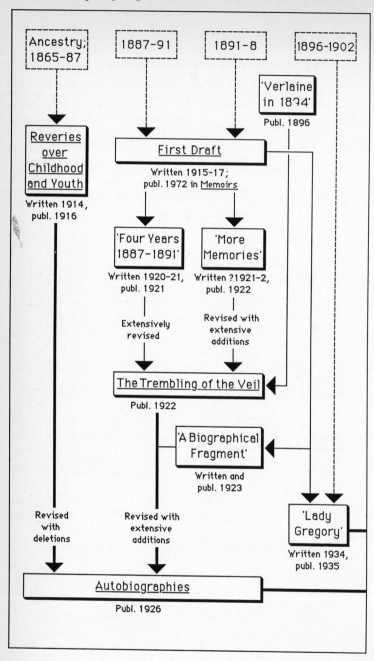

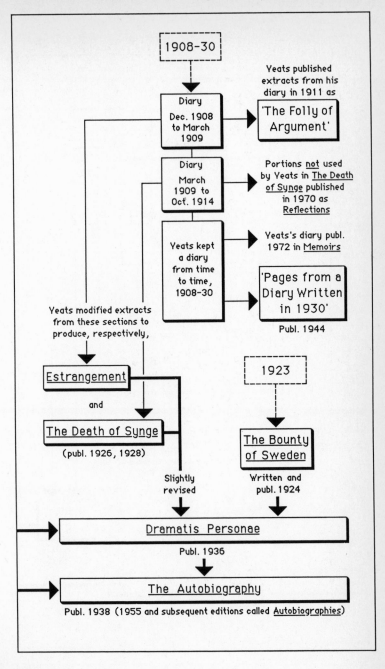

Bibliography

(This list excludes works by Yeats, and Wade's bibliography of Yeats's works and his edition of Yeats's letters. These appear, with bibliographical details, in the *List of Abbreviations*.)

Albright, Daniel. *The Myth against Myth: A Study of Yeats's Imagination in Old Age*. London: Oxford Univ. Press, 1972.

Bradford, Curtis. 'The Speckled Bird: A Novel by W. B. Yeats'. *Irish Writing*, 31 (1955), 9-18.

Bradford, Curtis. *Yeats at Work*. Carbondale: Southern Illinois Univ. Press, 1965.

Bruss, Elizabeth W. *Autobiographical Acts: The Changing Situation of a Literary Genre*. Baltimore: Johns Hopkins Univ. Press, 1976.

Coleridge, S. T. *Biographia Literaria*. Ed. James Engell and W. Jackson Bate. London: Routledge & Kegan Paul, 1983.

Culbertson, Diana. 'Twentieth-Century Autobiography: Yeats, Sartre, Nabokov: Studies in Structure and Form'. Diss. University of North Carolina at Chapel Hill 1971.

Davies, Joan. 'The Prose Style of W. B. Yeats's *Autobiography*'. Diss. University of Maryland 1981.

Eliot, T. S. *The Complete Poems and Plays of T. S. Eliot*. London: Faber & Faber, 1969.

Ellmann, Richard. *Eminent Domain: Yeats among Wilde, Joyce, Pound, Eliot and Auden*. New York: Oxford Univ. Press, 1967.

Ellmann, Richard. *Golden Codgers: Biographical Speculations*. New York: Oxford Univ. Press, 1973.

Ellmann, Richard. *The Identity of Yeats*. Rev. edn. New York: Oxford Univ. Press, 1964.

Ellmann, Richard. *Yeats: The Man and the Masks*. New York: Macmillan, 1948.

Fallon, Ann. 'Toward the Internalization of the Myth: Three Studies of W. B. Yeats's Revisions of His Unpublished Novel *The Speckled Bird*'. Diss. Brandeis University 1980.

Fleishman, Avrom. 'The Fictions of Autobiographical Fiction'. *Genre*, 9 (1976), 73-86.

Fleishman, Avrom. *Figures of Autobiography: The Language of Self-writing in Victorian and Modern England*. Berkeley: Univ. of California Press, 1983.

Fletcher, Ian. 'Rhythm and Pattern in *Autobiographies*'. In *An Honoured Guest: New Essays on W. B. Yeats.* Ed. Denis Donoghue and J. R. Mulryne. London: Edward Arnold, 1965, 165-89.

Genet, Jacqueline. *William Butler Yeats: Les fondements et l'évolution de la création poétique.* N.p.: Université de Lille, 1976.

Gide, André. *Si le grain ne meurt.* Paris: Gallimard, 1928.

Goldknopf, David. *The Life of the Novel.* Chicago: Univ. of Chicago Press, 1972.

Harper, G. M., ed. *Yeats and the Occult.* Toronto: Macmillan, 1975.

Hart, Francis R. 'Notes for an Anatomy of Modern Autobiography'. *New Literary History,* 1 (1970), 485-511.

Hone, Joseph. *W. B. Yeats: 1865-1939.* Rev. edn. London: Macmillan, 1962.

Jeffares, A. Norman, *W. B. Yeats: Man and Poet.* London: Routledge & Kegan Paul, 1962.

Jeffares, A. Norman. and K. G. W. Cross, edd. *In Excited Reverie: A Centenary Tribute to William Butler Yeats, 1865-1939.* London: Macmillan, 1965.

Joyce, James. *A Portrait of the Artist as a Young Man.* Ed. Chester G. Anderson. New York: Viking Press, 1968.

Kazin, Alfred. 'Autobiography as Narrative'. *Michigan Quarterly Review,* 3 (1964), 210-16.

Kenner, Hugh. *A Colder Eye: The Modern Irish Writers.* New York: Knopf, 1983.

Mandel, B. J. 'The Autobiographer's Art'. *Journal of Aesthetics and Art Criticism,* 27 (1968), 215-26.

Mansell, Darrel. 'Unsettling the Colonel's Hash: "Fact" in Autobiography'. *Modern Language Quarterly,* 37 (1976), 115-32.

Mazlish, Bruce. 'Autobiography and Psycho-analysis'. *Encounter,* 35, 4 (October 1970), 28-37.

Murphy William M. *Prodigal Father: The Life of John Butler Yeats (1839-1922).* Ithaca: Cornell Univ. Press, 1978.

Murphy, William M. 'William Butler Yeats's *John Sherman:* An Irish Poet's Declaration of Independence'. *Irish University Review,* 9 (1979), 92-111.

Nabokov, Vladimir. 'Pouchkine, ou le vrai et le vraisemblable'. *Nouvelle Revue Française,* 48 (1937), 362-78.

Nabokov, Vladimir. *Speak, Memory.* Rev. edn. New York: Putnam, 1966.

Nabokov, Vladimir. *Strong Opinions.* New York: McGraw Hill, 1973.

Neuman, Shirley. *Some One Myth: Yeats's Autobiographical Prose.* Portlaoise: Dolmen Press, 1982.

O'Brien, Kevin. 'Will and Reverie: The Personae of W. B. Yeats's Autobiography'. Diss. Fordham University 1972.

O'Hara, Daniel T. *Tragic Knowledge: Yeats's Autobiography and Hermeneutics.* New York: Columbia Univ. Press, 1981.

O'Hara, Daniel T. 'Under the Watch-mender's Eye: The Simplifying Image of the Creator in *The Autobiography* of William Butler Yeats'. Diss. Temple University 1976.

Olney, James. *Metaphors of Self: The Meaning of Autobiography.* Princeton: Princeton Univ. Press, 1972.

Olney, James, ed. *Autobiography: Essays Theoretical and Critical.* Princeton: Princeton Univ. Press, 1980.

Pascal, Roy. 'The Autobiographical Novel and the Autobiography'. *Essays in Criticism,* 9 (1959), 134-50.

Pascal, Roy. *Design and Truth in Autobiography.* London: Routledge & Kegan Paul, 1960.

Perloff, Marjorie. '"The Tradition of Myself": The Autobiographical Mode of Yeats'. *Journal of Modern Literature,* 4 (1975), 529-73.

Pilling, John. *Autobiography and Imagination: Studies in Self-scrutiny.* London: Routledge & Kegan Paul, 1981.

Pirri, John. 'William Butler Yeats and Symbolic Autobiography'. Diss. University of Wisconsin 1972.

Poirier, Richard. *The Performing Self: Compositions and Decompositions in the Languages of Contemporary Life.* New York: Oxford Univ. Press, 1971.

Renza, Louis A. 'The Veto of the Imagination: A Theory of Autobiography'. Diss. University of California at Irvine 1972.

Renza, Louis A. 'The Veto of the Imagination: A Theory of Autobiography'. *New Literary History,* 9 (1977), 1-26.

Ronsley, Joseph. 'Yeats as an Autobiographical Poet'. In Joseph Ronsley, ed., *Myth and Reality in Irish Literature.* Waterloo, Ont.: Wilfrid Laurier Univ. Press, 1977, 129-48.

Ronsley, Joseph. *Yeats's Autobiography: Life as Symbolic Pattern.* Cambridge, Mass.: Harvard Univ. Press, 1968.

Scholes, Robert, and Robert Kellogg. *The Nature of Narrative.* London: Oxford Univ. Press, 1966.

Shapiro, Stephen A. 'The Dark Continent of Literature: Autobiography'. *Comparative Literature Studies,* 5 (1968), 421-54.

Shaw, W. David. '*In Memoriam* and the Rhetoric of Confession'. *ELH,* 38 (1971), 80-103.

Shumaker, Wayne. *English Autobiography: Its Emergence, Materials, and Form.* Berkeley: Univ. of California Press, 1954.

Spender, Stephen. 'Confessions and Autobiography'. In *The Making of a Poem.* London: Hamish Hamilton, 1955, 63-72.

Spender, Stephen. *World within World.* London: Hamish Hamilton, 1951.

Spengemann, William C. *The Forms of Autobiography: Episodes.in the History of a Literary Genre.* New Haven: Yale Univ. Press, 1980.

Weintraub, Karl J. 'Autobiography and Historical Consciousness'. *Critical Inquiry*, 1 (1975), 821-48.

Wilson, F. A. C. *Yeats's Iconography*. London: Gollancz, 1960.

Wright, G. T. *The Poet in the Poem: The Personae of Eliot, Yeats and Pound.* Berkeley: Univ. of California Press, 1960.

Yeats, J. B. *Early Memories: Some Chapters of Autobiography*. Dundrum: Cuala Press, 1923.

Yeats, J. B. *J. B. Yeats: Letters to His Son, W. B. Yeats, and Others, 1869-1922*. Ed. Joseph Hone. London: Faber & Faber, 1944.

Index

For main entries page numbers are given in bold type